INDEX

BRAD POWER's
Best Seller Books
in Kindle edition and Paperback

- *Mossad and Saudi "hand in hand" against IRAN*
- *ISIS: Saudi Intel Dirty War*
- *Hillary Clinton for President? Not in my Name*
- *Bin Laden's Top Secret Files*
- *Erdogan-Gulen: The End Game*
- *Hassan Nasrallah: Leader or Terrorism*
- *Tsipras: Europe's Chavez*

Hamas and Hezbollah

Hamas is an acronym for Harakat al-Muqawamah al-Islamiyyah (Islamic Resistance Movement). Founded in 1987, Hamas is a militant Sunni Palestinian organization operating primarily in the Gaza Strip and parts of the West Bank. The group's followers are opposed to the existence of Israel, and believe that it is the religious duty of every Muslim to assist in the return of all Israeli-controlled territory to the Palestinians. Hamas is part militant fighting force, part Sunni political party and part social service organization that has a growing influence in its OE.

An overarching Shura council provides organizational guidance and over-sight for the organization as a whole. Hamas is composed of three overlapping "wings" or sections—the social services/welfare section, the political bureau and the military wing. The political bureau is led by Khalad Mashal. Mashal's deputy, Mousa Abu Marzouk, operates in the Gaza Strip.

The political bureau, which is the public political face of Hamas, is composed of 8-12 members and oversees the combat elements (Qassam Brigades) and social services section. Despite public pronouncements of such organizational boundaries, the divisions are operationally less significant. Missions, personnel and resources flow between the sections with the military component ultimately garnering the most attention and funding. The fighting section, as the group's name states, defines it is the heart and soul of Hamas.

Although categorized as a non-state actor, in many respects Hamas acts like a traditional political party by providing public services and social programs to the local population and participating in the Palestinian political process. On January 25, 2006, Hamas won 74 out of 132 seats in the Palestinian parliamentary election and the following year it seized power from Fatah in the Gaza Strip in a bloody coup d'état. Today, Hamas is the dominant political, social, economic and military force operating in Gaza.

Hezbollah, whose name means "Party of God," is the older of the two organizations, being founded in 1982. The group's objectives include the establishment of a Shiite theocracy in Lebanon, the destruction of Israel, and the elimination of western influences from the Middle East. The US Director of National Intelligence (DNI), retired Admiral Dennis Blair, defines Hezbollah as "a multifaceted, disciplined organization that combines political, social, paramilitary and terrorist elements."

The DNI also foresees that "in any potential future conflict, Hezbollah is likely to be better prepared and more capable than in 2006" as it continues to adapt and hone its fighting skills and incorporate lessons learned from its past engagements. Over the decades, Hezbollah has not only professionalized its military capabilities but joined Lebanon's political process and enmeshed itself into the fabric of Lebanese society.

Like Hamas, Hezbollah is a global entity, but Hezbollah's reach and depth of operations is more developed. Hezbollah's global presence is amplified by its substantial Iranian political and financial support. Iran supports both groups, but Hezbollah is clearly favored due to the fact that the founding of Hezbollah was one of revolutionary Iran's first acts, their shared Shia adherence, and importantly, Hezbollah's successes. The current intelligence community position is that "Hezbollah" is the largest recipient of Iranian financial aid, training, and weaponry, and Iran's senior leadership has cited Hezbollah as a model for other militant groups. With this backing, Hezbollah has successfully established its presence across to the globe, including the United States.

From the outside the groups appear similar as radical Islamic elements seeking political cover for their military aspirations. Both are trained and supplied by the key regional powers of Iran and Syria. Indeed, the groups share traits across the political, military, economic and social spectrum. Though non-state actors, both groups have become a "state-within-a-state", taking advantage of weak and corrupt local governments to advance their political, economic, and military aims. Both groups have stepped into broken societies to provide basic services such as health care, food aid, employment opportunities, and the construction of mosques and schools.

Consequently they have been rewarded with elected positions in their host governments and widespread admiration in the Ummah (the Muslim world or "community of believers"). Despite their adherence to differing religious doctrine, the Sunni Hamas and Shia Hezbollah work together by sharing financial resources, equipment and tactics.

Hamas has become much more than a military force, weaving itself into key positions across Gazan society. It seeks to gain legitimacy as a political belligerent in both Gaza and the West Bank. Hamas joined the political process when it entered the Palestinian parliamentary election in 2006. The organization was not seeking to create a Palestinian state in the Gaza Strip, but rather sought to form an Islamic state to replace Israel.

In 2007 a Palestinian National Unity Government was formed under Hamas leader Ismail Haniya. Later that year Hamas "succeeded in a violent takeover of all military and governmental institutions in the Gaza Strip", the aforementioned coup. However, as a Center for Strategic and International Studies (CSIS) report notes, "this victory occurred far more because of a lack of leadership and elementary competence on the part of the Fatah/Palestinian Authority Forces than any great skill on the part of Hamas."

As a current IDF Colonel explains: *"There really isn't any alternative to Hamas. Fatah is a proven failure and at least Hamas is attempting reconstruction with Iranian money versus stealing it like Fatah did."* Hamas shrewdly capitalized on Fatah's weaknesses, the Israeli political paralysis and Western blindness, and successfully convinced the Gazan population it could provide needed political and economic improvements. Hamas saw a political opportunity and seized it.

Hamas, whose political control extends only over the Gaza Strip, uses both social and religious programs to solidify its political legitimacy. However, support for Hamas in the Gaza Strip isn't as strong as it sometimes appears: a January 2009 report reveals: *"on the streets of Gaza, support for Hamas remains strong, but in private, expressions of anger, fear and exhaustion are heard."*

The cause of this frustration may stem from the death and destruction in Gaza caused by the recent conflict with Israel combined with Hamas' inability to improve the living conditions of Gazans. Unlike Hezbollah in southern Lebanon, Hamas appears not to have made the transition "from Islamic governance to good governance."

As public support for Hamas has withered in Gaza, political unity within the group is also faltering. While Hamas leadership claims cohesion, there is evidence of increasing and significant political tension within the organization. According to the Washington Institute for Near East Policy, friction exists *"between the groups' internal leadership on the ground in the Palestinian territories and its external leadership, between leaders in the West Bank and those in Gaza, and between religious Palestinian nationalists and radical Islamists."*

While most day-to-day decisions are made by the leadership in Qatar they now face increasing resistance from the leaders in Gaza. Deputy Mousa Abu Marzouk's "more moderate stance" is perceived as creating a rift between himself and his boss, Meshal.

This difference of opinion may be causing a lack of clear or timely guidance from the highest levels of leadership and may have negatively affected Hamas' ability to act during its recent combat with Israel. However, according to Matthew Levitt of the Washington Institute for Near East Policy, *the most significant fault line with Hamas is between those who prioritize the Palestinian national cause and those who prioritize the group's Islamist ideology.*

This tension may prove to be the most troublesome for Hamas as it attempts to be both a legitimate political force and terrorist organization. Politically, Hamas has been successful at gaining power, but the question remains whether it can translate this into the political capital in Gaza and the West Bank to follow a more extremist path.

By comparison, Hezbollah appears to have a much more unified leadership—or is, at the very least, able to keep such dissension private. This Shia-dominated political party and militant organization has actively participated in Lebanon's political system since 1992.

Like Hamas, it has muscled itself in key posts across Lebanese society. According to one analysis, "Hezbollah can be active on four tracks simultaneously—the political, the social, the guerilla, and the terrorist—because its Iranian leaders are masters of long-term strategic subversion." Like Hamas, Hezbollah skillfully uses social and religious programs and economic aid to gain popular support and establish political legitimacy.

Sayyed Hassan Nasrallah is Hezbollah's Secretary General and seems to enjoy uncontested power. Numbers vary, but most estimates claim that Hezbollah has up to 10,000 active members and 30,000 supporters. As mentioned, Iran directly influences the political and military decision-making and strategic agenda of both Hezbollah and Hamas. However, as Hezbollah has matured and become dominant as a Lebanese political party, there is some question concerning the depth to which Iran is now able to sway Hezbollah's political decisions and military strategies. However, even if Iranian influence is dwindling in Lebanon, Iran and Syria remain key partners of both Hamas and Hezbollah and will continue to use each other for mutual benefit.

The Second Lebanon War

The 2006 conflict was triggered by successive Hezbollah attempts to kidnap Israeli soldiers for use as hostages or bartered in exchanges for terrorists held in Israel. It had made several previous attempts to kidnap IDF soldiers when its fifth attempt, on 12 July 2006, succeeded. Under covering fire, including ATGMs, a Hezbollah team crossed into Israel and snatched two IDF soldiers, then exfiltrated back to Lebanese territory.

Within days, Israeli Prime Minister Ehud Olmert declared the Hezbollah abduction an act of war and the stage was set for the 34-day long conflict between Hezbollah and Israel. Hezbollah's strategy in the conflict was simple; it would focus strategically and operationally on continuing its rocket fire into Israel and attempt to weaken Israeli resolve while defending from its well-prepared positions in southern Lebanon.

This supports Hezbollah's IO message that victory comes from the willingness to stand and fight a dominant opponent. This message has great currency in the Arab and Muslim world. Knowing Israel's sensitivity toward casualties, Hezbollah's Islamic Resistance would attempt to attrit Israeli forces as they advanced across southern Lebanon. Hezbollah used a combined-arms approach against the IDF and Israeli populace as well as the world audience to leverage its strengths.

Israel's response was initially focused on air strikes by the Israeli Air Force (IAF) with ground forces added to the mix toward the end of the conflict. Israel suffered 119 soldiers and 43 civilians killed and an estimated 300,000 (a staggering 20%) of its residents were displaced during the conflict. In the end, a total of 4,000 rockets rained on Israel, resulting in one-third of the population being exposed to the terrifying rocket attacks.

Hezbollah claims that it lost 250 fighters killed while Israeli estimates indicate the number maybe closer to 600. Ultimately, many analysts have concluded that Hezbollah was successful in turning the conflict into a loss for Israel even though there were no decisive battles, no clear winners and no clear losers. While Hezbollah claimed victory, Israel began to analyze its mistakes.

Hezbollah TTPs

A review of past Hezbollah TTPs shows that the group—like Hamas—has conducted a range of attacks. These include indirect fire attacks, primarily with rocket and mortar; direct fire attacks (anti-armor and surface-to-air fire), employed explosives, IEDs/explosively-formed penetrator (EFP) and mines, and conducted raids, ambushes and kidnappings. Despite its lack of air power and armor, Hezbollah engaged Israeli forces in a major combat operation. In the 34-day war, Hezbollah fought in small, dispersed and shielded units utilizing "hit-and-run" tactics that denied IAF targets and limited Israel's ISR effectiveness.

Unlike Hamas, which suffered decapitation and degradation on the first day from massive Israeli air strikes, Hezbollah did not suffer such an overwhelmingly devastating attack. Israeli targeting in Lebanon focused on Lebanese civilian infrastructure, such radio and television stations and airports, rather than Hezbollah infrastructure. According to one Israeli commentator, the most important lesson that Israel learned during its Hezbollah conflict was that, "in the face of enemies who have opted for a strategy of attrition and attacking from a distance, Israel will present itself as a 'crazy country', the kind that will respond in a massive and unfettered assault, with no proportion to the amount of casualties it has endured."

Hezbollah was very successful in cover and concealment, preparation of its fighting positions, and its coordination of direct fire support. However, despite such success, mistakes were made. Hezbollah deficiencies include controlling maneuver forces, integrating indirect fire and movement and small arms marksmanship. To put this into historical perspective, despite Hezbollah's weaknesses, it scored more "Israeli causalities per Arab fighter in 2006 than did any of Israel's state opponents in 1956, 1967, 1973, or the 1982 Arab-Israeli interstate wars." And it forced Israel to rethink its doctrine and strategy.

Operational Shielding

Both Hezbollah and Hamas understand the value of operational shielding. Both groups utilize "hugging" or hiding tactics designed to force Israel to abstain from attacking due to fears of collateral causalities. Hezbollah fighters tried to blend in with the civilian populations and use residential structures for firing positions and hide-outs while Hezbollah's leader Hassan Nasrallah is thought to have commanded the Second Lebanon War from the Iranian Embassy in Beirut. Videotapes show Hezbollah placed rocket launchers in firing positions next to residential buildings or hidden inside garages between fire missions.

Rocket launchers were also dispersed into urban settings to maximize operational shielding. The Israeli counter-fire missions were limited due to the fear of increasing civilian causalities. Hezbollah's ability to "exploit virtually any built up area and familiar terrain as fortresses or ambush sites at least partially compensated for IDF armor, air mobility, superior firepower, and sensors."

Hezbollah used civilians as human shields and civilian homes to conceal launchers and as direct fire combat positions. Hezbollah also fired rocket launchers from within buildings and homes. Hezbollah fighters blended in with the population effectively. Some did use civilian clothing for deception; however, many wore military uniforms.

There are even examples of IDF soldiers hesitating to fire on Hezbollah fighters "because their kit, from a distance, looked so much like the IDF infantry's." Hezbollah combat engineers constructed excellent defensive positions. Numerous strong points were dispersed across the towns of southern Lebanon. Outposts were constructed in rural areas for security and intelligence operations. The IDF reported finding over 500 weapon caches and hundreds of mobile rocket/missile sites across this well-defended area.

This dispersed-yet-integrated defense was composed of primarily company-size strong points (including primary, secondary and decoy positions). Hezbollah was well prepared to fight IDF units. Nasrallah apparently planned to deter Israel from deep attacks into Lebanon with his rocket forces and limit and exhaust any Israeli ground operations with his defensive systems in the south, which was based on ATGMs and well-hidden and protected fighters.

Hezbollah built launch sites for both its short-range and medium-range rockets throughout southern Lebanon. Many of these were built into the ground, using pneumatic lifts to raise and lower the launchers from under-ground shelters. Many were launched from trucks positioned as stand-alone launchers. Firing teams sought protection in nearby bunkers and caves to hide from IDF counter-battery attacks.

Hezbollah often participated in extended direct firefights with the IDF. One excellent example is the fight at outpost Shaked. At this location, a "dug-in Hezbollah defensive position remained in place on a critical hillcrest near the Israeli border between Avivim and Marun ar Ras, exchanging fire with IDF tanks and infantry for more than 12 hours before finally being destroyed in place by Israeli fire."

Again at Marun ar Ras, Hezbollah defenders fought room-to-room with IDF soldiers holding their positions for close to 7 hours; at Bint Jbeil, Hezbollah fighters battled IDF units for 4 days after which the IDF forces retrograded and executed bombing strikes. Clearly, these cases—and numerous others not cited—show that Hezbollah has the capability to sustain the close-in, direct-fire fight. Hezbollah also succeeded in conducting counterattacks against the IDF at the platoon level or smaller, although examples of this are less common.

In situations where IDF units were able to clear Hezbollah fighters from their defensive positions, they infiltrated back and quickly reestablished their positions once the IDF units moved on or withdrew. Hezbollah showed that it possessed the ability to tactically maneuver under fire and hold ground while conducting limited maneuver operations.

Hezbollah gave Israel a substantial infantry and anti-armor fight and showed skills in tactically hiding, moving and dispersing. Hezbollah was able to maintain a steady stream of Katyusha rockets throughout the entire conflict. Both Hezbollah and Hamas used rockets as their primary strategic and operational fires response to the IDF. Hezbollah's rock-ets represented excellent "psychological and political weapons with strategic affect."

Hezbollah launched close to 4,000 rockets with more than 200 rockets per day fired into Israel during the final days of the war. As noted, Hezbollah's rocket inventory included the long-range Iranian-made Zelzal -2, Nazeat, Fajr-3, and the Fajr-5, but the significant majority (80-90%) of its rocket inventory consisted of the shorter-range, proven Katyusha rockets. Whether or not Hezbollah possessed the capability to adjust the fire of these area-fire weapons is academic as the vast majority simply rained down on Israeli citizens.

Perhaps the most important difference between Hezbollah and Hamas' artillery capability was in the ability to integrate fires. Hezbollah successfully integrated anti-armor fires with indirect fires, providing cover for reposition and subsequent anti-armor engagements.

Hezbollah was also able to successfully separate and isolate Israeli infantry and supporting armor units. In addition, Hezbollah surprised Israeli forces with a new strike capability—the C-802 anti-ship missile. On July 14, 2006 Hezbollah fired two of these missiles at the INS Hanit, causing significant damage. Hezbollah leaders coupled this surprise attack capability with sophisticated media exploitation.

Moments prior to the strike, Nasrallah went on al-Manar TV and provided a live countdown to the strike. As the missile was launched, he confidently suggested that viewers in Beirut look toward the west for a spectacular sight. The timing of the broadcast was impeccable and serving as a lethal theatrical drum roll. This is an excellent example of Hezbollah's ability to use its media and information prowess as a combat multiplier as well as highlighting its flair for the dramatic that results in a massive IO victory.

In the direct-fire close fighting Hezbollah employed ATGMs by anti-armor teams of 5-6 fighters. Typically the teams allowed IDF tanks to pass by and then engaged them from the rear. Hezbollah fighters fired ATGMs at buildings that IDF soldiers had used to shelter from small-arms and mortar fire. These tandem-warhead missiles either penetrated deeply into the buildings' interiors or collapsed them. Although very few Israeli tanks suffered a catastrophic ATGM hit, many IDF tanks were damage and taken out of action.

Hezbollah's ATGM armory could boast of advanced missiles like the AT-14E Kornet missile, which reportedly "took a considerable toll on Israeli armor in the confused, sporadic ground war that raged close to the border."

Hezbollah also employed the RPG 29, the AT-4 Spigot, the AT-5 Spandrel, and the AT-13 METIS-M. Final estimates indicate that 40 tanks were damaged, *"resulting in the deaths of 30 tank crewmen—25 percent of the IDF's entire combat losses in the war."* These losses, especially with regard to the sophisticated Israeli Merkava tank, constituted another Hezbollah IO victory.

Hezbollah used IEDs and land mines across southern Lebanon. "Explosive pits" and EFPs were emplaced along main roads in southern Lebanon. Coupled with rocket attacks, this ordinance limited the IDF's ability to maneuver.

In addition, Hezbollah's minefield employment was sometimes tied into direct fire defensive systems in a systematic way and sometimes not. However, there are examples of the use of mines coupled with "obstacles over-watched by fires," evidence of Hezbollah's sophistication.

Hezbollah acted as a 'distributed network' of small cells and units acting with considerable independence, and capable of rapidly adapting to local conditions rather than having to react faster than the IDF's decision cycle, they could largely ignore it, waiting out Israeli attacks, staying in positions, re-infiltrating or reemerging from cover, and choosing the time to attack or ambush."

An additional Hezbollah strength was its ability to maintain communications throughout the conflict, while intercepting and exploiting Israeli communications. Hezbollah's ability to listen to, and locate, cell phone traffic had been a major problem [for Israel] in the fighting with Hezbollah. Hezbollah's excellent, diverse, and hard-to-target capabilities included fiber-optic landlines, cell phones, secure radio, messengers, the internet and the al-Manar television station.

Hezbollah controlled the information environment and integrated kinetic operations into its strategic IO. The organization has conducted some of the most successful information operations in the Middle East by employing many experts specializing in psychological warfare and propaganda, operating its own television, radio, and internet sites and collaborating with supporting media (such as that owned by like-minded Islamists). Hezbollah focused on Lebanese civilian casualties and infrastructure damage. Hezbollah accomplished this by performing sophisticated editing and photo and video manipulation, presenting a skewed picture of the war's progress.

Media exploitation was one of Hezbollah's most effective weapons. According to one source, Hezbollah's IO motto could be summed up as, "if you haven't captured it on film—you haven't fought." Ultimately, all of Hezbollah's battlefield successes integrated into its overall IO plan—its greatest victory of the war being the destruction of the myth of Israel's battlefield invincibility. In the end, Hezbollah survived, and gained increased international and regional recognition of its military capabilities and warfighting skills.

A cursory review of these conflicts shows Hezbollah is capable of tactical actions that are much more complex than a typical non-state belligerent. They show sophistication and the clear ability to conduct major combat operations. Hezbollah's use of effective TTPs, mastery of the terrain and ability to simulta-neously negate Israel's advantages (mobility and air supremacy) proved more successful and gave Israel a surprisingly harder fight with strategic conse-quences. As the next section will show, Hamas has learned much from Hezbol-lah, through Hezbollah-sponsored training, weapons assistance, and adoption of similar TTPs.

2008 war against Hamas

In April 2008, the IDF declared a significant and increasing threat from Hamas after months of receiving rocket and mortar fire from the Gaza Strip. An Israeli statement claimed that threats from Hamas *"include improved capabilities to carry out complex terrorist attacks such as mass-casualty attacks and the abduction of soldiers and civilians; an increase in the scope, accuracy, range and force of rocket fire into Israel and increasing the threat of anti-tank weapons to Israel's tanks and armored vehicles and to IDF soldiers."*

Two months later, following a period of growing tension, Israel and Hamas established a six-month truce, mandating that Hamas cease rocket fire against Israel and Israel end its economic blockade on Gaza. Neither Hamas nor the Israelis completely honored this cease-fire; rocket fire did not stop and the supplies into Gaza were not adequate to pull Gaza out of its growing economic and humanitarian crises. In December 2008 both parties failed to agree on conditions to extend the truce and the Hamas/Israeli conflict ignited on 19 December 2008.

The conflict, known as Operation CAST LEAD to the Israelis, began with a massive Israeli air strike against Hamas high-value targets (HVTs) across the Gaza Strip. Operation CAST LEAD, which was intended to stop the harassing Hamas rocket attacks on Israel, lasted more than three weeks. In the end, Hamas estimates, more than 4,000 homes were destroyed and 17,000 others damaged during the campaign,104 with recent estimates indicating that 1,417 people (including 255 police officers and 236 Hamas fighters) were killed.

The Israeli perception was that Hamas was taken by surprise.106 However, two days prior to the air strike, senior Hamas leaders were reportedly moving into hiding, and key Hamas materials and computers were being moved to different locations. Hamas fighters left their bases, and according to an International Crisis Group observation, police forces chose to "operate outside of their stations for the sake of self-protection at night, when IDF attacks were most likely." Israel may have surprised Hamas with the scope of its initial air attack, but

Hamas was clearly preparing for some type of Israeli action. Perhaps, as a CSIS report suggests, "like the Hezbollah's leader in 2006, Hamas fundamentally mischaracterized its enemy in terms of both its intentions and Prior to the conflict, a Qassam Brigade spokesman said Hamas was con-fident in its ability to conduct both offensive and defensive operations against the IDF. "Our defense plan is based, to a great extent, on rockets which have not yet been used and on a network of ditches and tunnels dug under a large area of the Strip. The [Israeli] army will be surprised when it sees fighters coming up out of the ground and engaging it with unexpected equipment and weapons."

Those capabilities, if not overstated, were greatly underutilized— resulting in Hamas failing to achieve its goals against Israeli forces. Reviews of past Hamas actions show that the group is capable of conducting a wide variety of attacks including indirect and direct fire attacks, raids, ambushes/kidnappings and the employment of IEDs/mines. In terms of defending Gaza against Israel, Hamas apparently wanted to "wage a guerilla war of attrition, especially in densely populated built-up areas"—a strategy drawing almost exclusively from the Hezbollah 2006 game plan.

The tactical plan was to draw Israel deep into Gaza and attack IDF units with small-arms and ATGM fire. If successful, Hamas would draw IDF units into killing zones and inflict significant causalities, eroding Israel's willingness to continue the fight. At the operational level, Hamas planned to use rocket and mortar attacks as a show of force and continue to harass the population of Israel.

Again, pulling from lessons learned in the 2006 conflict, Hamas obviously attempted to use many of Hezbollah's common TTPs. These included rocket attacks to inflict politically unacceptable Israeli casualties, "hit-and-run" di-rect engagement attacks followed by dispersion into small units, and fighting from inside civilian structures with the ultimate aim of executing their attrition IDF Commander Colonel Halevy claimed that Hamas' "forces were di-vided into six territorial brigades (operating in the four sectors previously mentioned), each tasked with defending a specific sector of Gaza. There are indications that the majority of the brigades were composed largely of local fighters. Each brigade consisted of three battalions, which were organized into company and platoons, composed by the core group of fighters supplement-ed with local manpower.

Hamas used the urban terrain to its advantage in terms of providing cover and operational and tactical shielding. It placed fighters and weapon cach-es inside schools, mosques, and other public buildings in addition to homes.

In preparation, Hamas booby-trapped houses and buildings, placed IEDs in homes, and used its tunnel network to move and resupply, albeit not as effectively as Hezbollah. Hamas used Gaza's main hospital as a command center and defensive fighting position.

Hamas used the Hezbollah model and built up defensive positions in urban areas—and, as one report states, Hamas promised to turn Gaza "into a grave-yard for Israeli forces." It boldly announced that "the Zionist enemy will see surprises and will regret carrying out such an operation and will pay a heavy price."

Hamas fighters, however, were unable to achieve the majority of their defensive goals; many Hamas fighters simply fled, or hid, while others were killed by effective Israeli fires. The one success was its ability to continue to fire rockets at Israel throughout the operation, although Israel degraded this capability by suppressing or overrunning the launch sites. At the beginning of the conflict, Hamas launched up to 80 rockets each day, but that number was reduced to no more than 20 at the end. In contrast, Hezbollah fired more than 200 rockets per day throughout its Israeli conflict.

Some close combat fighting did occur, but "sustained ground fighting was limited, and Hamas protected itself by avoiding direct engagements." Like Hezbollah, Hamas favored "hit-and-run" tactics, dispersing quickly to avoid IDF counterattacks. The IDF, though, was able to move quickly, use urban cover and conduct "suppressive fire to deny Hamas the ability to repeat the kind of successful short range strikes and swarming of multiple firing of such weapons that Hezbollah had carried out in 2006."

Hamas' defenses appear to have folded and the fighters quickly dispersed back into the civilian popula-tion. The strategy to draw the Israelis deep into Gaza and attack with strong resistance had failed.117 As discussed earlier, IDF soldiers were surprised by this lack of resistance and the overall low quality of the Hamas fighters in contrast to the performances of the "village fighters" of Hezbollah.

Hamas typically relied upon indirect rocket attacks and small arms fire. Overall, Hamas failed to surprise the IDF with either its weaponry or tactics. There were no incidents like Hezbollah's surprise use of the C-802 anti-ship missile during the Hamas conflict. There was one report of an ATGM being used, but no information has been provided on its effectiveness. Reports also show that RPG-29s were used several times—with one penetrating an armored Israeli bulldozer. The IAF also reports that Hamas fired anti-aircraft missiles at it—probably the SA-7.

Given Hamas' stated goal of acquiring advanced ATGMs as part of its overall military build-up, why was there so little use of this capability? It was most likely a function of poorly trained and disciplined ATGMs gunners and lack of necessary cueing systems for targeting and effective IDF tactics (use of smoke, bypassing Hamas defensive positions, and maneuver at night). IDF troops surrounded and drove Hamas from many of its rocket-firing positions and into Gaza City, where the IDF was able to effectively eliminate much of the tactical threat with counter-fire.

IDF forces also destroyed many of Hamas' stockpiles and safe houses in earlier air strikes. As more information becomes available on Hamas' actions during this operation, more definitive analysis can be presented as to why options were or were not used. It simply may have been a choice Hamas leaders made to preserve their capabilities for another battle.

Hamas placed IEDs on most key streets and main intersections—even planting IEDs in satellite dishes at residential sites to be remotely detonated once IDF soldiers approached. IDF units reported finding caches of weap-ons—including large amounts of ammunition—in most of the buildings it searched in Gaza City. This prepositioning of weapons and supplies gave the Hamas fighters the ability to fire from one building, leave the weapons behind, walk the streets as a civilian, and then enter another building start fighting again.

Hamas planned to rely on its substantial stockpiles of rockets, small-arms and IEDs to deter and counter Israeli actions. However, IDF units were able to bypassed Hamas strong points and negate many of the IEDs and booby trapped buildings based upon excellent Israeli intelligence. One-third of all Gaza homes encountered by the IDF were booby-trapped.

Additionally, Hamas' cell phone network was degraded. As a result, Hamas commanders were forced to "cease most of their communication with field units," relying on messengers or walkie-talkies. A CSIS report supports the claim that IAF strikes significantly degraded Hamas command structure and communication capabilities.

Fighters tended to avoid direct engagements with the IDF and many chose not to fight. There is very limited reporting of aggressive Hamas coordinated direct actions. Only one report from BBC sources claimed that Hamas fighters ambushed and aggressively attacked IDF units during the early stages of its advance into Gaza City. Most reports asserted that Hamas tended to operate as fixed defensive units "with only 300 fighters" actually fighting against the IDF.

Israel assessed that Hamas' C2 capabilities were weak and ineffective and speculated that some of the rockets fired by Hamas post cease-fire were "only fired because of a breakdown in Hamas' capabilities." In addition, Israeli intelligence collection efforts were aided by the poor "communication disci-pline" of Hamas. It appears that superior Israeli intelligence/IPB (assisted greatly by Fatah informants) and an inferior Hamas system caused delays in command decisions and its fighters' actions.

Hamas also knows the value of IO campaigns, but its means and target audiences are significantly different. As stated earlier, Hamas' IO message at-tempts to portray the organization as the victim of overwhelming and unjustified Israeli actions. Hamas conducted a successful and integrated IO campaign utilizing a spectrum of tools including radio, TV, internet and, importantly, fighters at all echelons trained on the importance of IO— constantly scanning for exploitable opportunities.

While Hezbollah focused on the Arab and Mus-lim world as its target audience, Hamas targeted a more Western audience, with the overall goal of pressuring Israel to "stop the killing." Unlike the 2006 conflict, Israel was more sanitized and proactive in its response to Hamas IO messages and denial of information outlets to Hamas. For example, Israel did not allow foreign reporters access to Gaza, jammed and kinetically targeted Hamas media outlets and promoted the Israeli narrative via outlets such as YouTube.com.

YouTube messages were specifically targeted to US audiences, using IDF personnel speaking American English. In response to these Israeli initiatives, Hamas countered by courting sympathetic international groups and organizations especially in Europe.

This begs the question: were Hamas' military capabilities and skills over-blown, or was Hamas simply challenged by a superior force? There is no single answer. Undoubtedly, Israel learned valuable lessons from its 2006 en-gagement with Hezbollah and applied those lessons against Hamas. Clearly, the Israelis feel that their tactical maneuvers and early devastating air strikes effectively paralyzed Hamas forces, allowing them to control the fight. Just as important, Israeli operational thinking clearly stresses avoidance of the attrition battle.

To this end, Israeli forces moved quickly to their objectives, bypassing Hamas resistance. Additionally, Hamas' capabilities were not as ro-bust as originally thought. For example, clearly Hamas lacked the advanced skills—such as signal intelligence (SIGINT)—that enabled Hezbollah.

While Hamas retains the ability to conduct suicide bombings and rocket attacks, this is a smaller order of magnitude than conventionally fighting an opponent like the IDF. Hamas' critical deficiencies in training, basic combat skills, intelligence, resupply have all been highlighted and will require significant time and resources to correct.

Not surprisingly, Hamas took a different view of its performance—one based on classic Arabic thinking that victory belongs to the smaller force that survives against a superior military power. Yet, despite this early celebration, there is clear evidence that Hamas recognizes its flaws. In late January 2009, reports begin to surface that Hamas was conducting an internal review of its less-than-stellar performance. Additional reporting indicates that the Qassam Brigades and Hamas intelligence units have admitted shortcomings and are reviewing their actions.

In the end, Hamas performed poorly and was forced to accept a less-than-satisfactory ceasefire. Unlike Hezbollah, Hamas cannot claim any significant success in its fight against Israel. As one CSIS report concludes, "the end result was that Hamas initiated the conflict as a weak non-state belligerent that could launch rocket and mortar attacks on Israeli civilian and civil facilities over an extended period of time but had little other warfighting capa-bility other than using its own densely populated urban areas as barriers. It did so in part because it had no other real means of combat." And despite losses of equipment, supporting infrastructure and fighters, there is "little doubt that Hamas, like Hezbollah, will rise from the rubble to emerge as strong as ever and probably stronger."

While important lessons can be gained in any comparison of conflicts and forces in those conflicts, one must be careful not to draw them too quickly and too broadly. Looking at a belligerent through the lens of its unique OE allows for better analytical context of both the operation and belligerent. In the specific case of Israel and its enemies, the belligerents' responses to Israel's ground of-fensive were different—reflecting their OE, as well as their overall capabilities and level of sophistication. Israel, like many in the West, may have assumed that Hamas would present a Hezbollah-like fight, but such assumptions can be faulty, misleading and potentially dangerous.

According to a Washington Institute for Near East Policy analyst, *"It is always a mistake to lump these two movements together. Hezbollah deserves the title 'Islamic Resistance' as it actually fought battles of maneuver and assaulted Israeli fortified lines, while 'the resistance of Hamas' has always been fiction."* *In fact, Hezbollah fights such categorization and views itself as fiercely independent of Hamas. It is worth noting that Hezbollah did not get involved in the recent fight between Israel and Hamas—most likely because Hezbollah realized Hamas might not win and it did not want its hard-won 2006 victory tarnished".*

Stephen Biddle and Jeffrey Friedman of the Strategic Studies Institute argue that *"Hezbollah's skills in conventional warfighting were clearly imper-fect in 2006—but they were also well within the observed bounds of other state military belligerents in the Middle East and elsewhere, and significantly superior to many such states."*

Overall, Hamas was not as well-armed and supplied as Hezbollah. Hamas was unable to offer any effective resistance to the ground fight, while Hezbol-lah offered substantial resistance to Israeli forces and conducted successful operations against the IDF. Both groups were successful at bringing the conflict directly to the Israeli population. And both conflicts help to reveal Iran's destabilizing role in the region and its increasing influence in the Arab world. Hezbollah presented the Israelis with a well trained, well led and suitably equipped force with sufficient space to defend in depth.

Hamas was inad-equately trained and poorly led with little space to trade for producing Israeli casualties. In the case of the 2006 conflict, the Israelis underestimated the capabilities of Hezbollah and overestimated its capability to fight such an oppo-nent. Such miscalculation is a recipe for international humiliation. Conversely, as in the case of Hamas, an underequipped, ill trained and poorly commanded opponent can be an annoyance—but it will not stand long against significant national power. Hamas presented the Israelis with a poor imitation of Hezbollah and Hezbollah wisely stayed on the sideline and watched the events unfold.

Both actions reinforce—one positively and one negatively—the lesson that a well trained, disciplined and well equipped paramilitary force, can fight successfully against a national Army for a limited, possibly substantial, period of time.

The State of the region

The recent tensions on the Israel-Syria border, and the Sunni attacks in Sinai and Suez against the Egyptians may seem unrelated, but they actually have several factors in common. These attacks attest to the impending collapse of regimes and nations in the region, and prove that radical groups are ready to exploit this. Recent security events against Israeli soldiers on the northern border and against the Egyptian military in Sinai are seemingly unrelated, but it would still be wise to link them together.

The tensions on the Israel-Syria border began when a delegation of senior Iranian Revolutionary Guard commanders visited the Golan Heights. The "targeting" of that delegation resulted in Hezbollah's attack on IDF troops in Shebaa farms, in which two soldiers were killed and seven others were wounded. The attacks in Sinai and Suez, in which 25 Egyptian military personnel were killed and 58 others were wounded including civilians, security and medical personnel, were carried out by the Islamic State group's Egyptian wing.

The incident on the northern border was carried out by Shiites, and the attacks in Egypt were the work of Sunnis. Israel is their enemy in the north, and Egypt is their enemy in the south. Although these incidents were different, , they have several things in common – they attest to the disintegration of regional regimes and states, and prove that radical groups operating in areas where the actual regime has become defunct are waiting in the wings, ready to exploit this disintegration.

Cutting the Gaza Strip off from Sinai by creating a substantial buffer zone and razing the smuggling tunnels running between Egypt and Gaza, are part of the extensive Egyptian effort to curtail terrorism. Israel benefits from these efforts, but Cairo is motivated solely by Egyptian interests.

Israel's alleged strike in Syria bears the same characteristics. Since Iran and Hezbollah are trying to exploit the governmental vacuum in the area, the strike was meant to clarify that there are red lines, and anyone crossing them must take into account that Israel will respond.

A preemptive strike meant to generate deterrence has its risks and therefore may come with a price. This was the case on the northern border, when

Hezbollah retaliated over a move attributed to Israel. It had to do so to save face after the public blow it was dealt the week before, but its method of choice – an attack in an area devoid any civilian communities, and against a military convoy – indicates caution. Hezbollah has no interest in an escalation and it has done everything in its power to prevent one, despite its inevitable response.

The fundamental elements at the heart of Hezbollah's prudence have remained unchanged. The war it is fighting is Syria has strategic, even existential, importance for the Shiite organization, as without Syria at its back it would struggle to sustain itself in Lebanon. Syria is Hezbollah's link to Iran, and all the aid the Islamic republic lends it arrived in Lebanon via Syria. Damascus itself is responsible for a considerable part of Hezbollah's military capabilities, and Hezbollah knows that as far as Beirut is concerned, it has no right to drag the Lebanese people into a war that is the result of its exploits in Syria. Regional realities have become less predictable and more violent than before, and their dynamics are changing much more rapidly.

Iran's strategy in Syria

Many Israeli military strategists point to a number of alarming indicators suggesting that Hezbollah may be stronger than it has ever been. And that has them worried. The massive arsenal of advanced weaponry Hezbollah has amassed since it last faced off with Israel in the 2006 Second Lebanon War, the technological advances it has made, and the battlefield experience it has gained in Syria, have all helped turn Hezbollah into what could be Israel's most dangerous enemy in a generation.

As a highly disciplined Islamist group that operates as an asymmetric terror and guerrilla force, a political party, and a mini-state in southern Lebanon, Hezbollah has of course been a serious threat to Israel for decades. As expressed in its 1985 "Open Letter," Hezbollah believes that an open-ended holy war—a jihad—is the "cure to the ills and oppression afflicted on Lebanon and the region by Israel." Put simply, Hezbollah has always seen Israel as an existential enemy that must be destroyed for both political and religious reasons.

Yet while the group's mission hasn't changed, its strategic significance has. Because of its location on Israel's northern border, Hezbollah has been a serious headache for the IDF since Israel withdrew from Lebanon in 2000; along with the group's attempt to corrupt Israeli society by smuggling drugs across the border, a source of both revenue and intelligence. And its evident subordination to Tehran has meant that Iran has now established a substantial military presence in both Syria and Lebanon, combining with the Syrian army and the IRGC to create what Israeli military officials now see as a single northern front across Syria and Lebanon, rendering previous security doctrines and realities obsolete.

For all intents and purposes, Iran is now sitting on Israel's northern border, making the Iranian nuclear threat a lot more immediate for Israeli decision-makers. If military grade missiles, rockets and unmanned aircraft systems are making their way into Hezbollah's hands, it is not difficult to imagine tactical nukes and dirty bombs aimed directly at Israel's northern civilian population. But even without nuclear weapons, Hezbollah may have already strengthened to the point that it is the most difficult enemy facing Israel today.

As the Assad regime is losing its grip over the country, Iran and Hezbollah gain a greater ability to establish a new base of operations against Israel in southern Syria. As the status quo is changing along Israel's northern border, Assad's fall may be useful to Israel's strategic interest to weaken Iran which is ideologically committed to the destruction of Israel and is trying to establish a new operations stage against Israel on the Syrian side of the Golan Heights – something that Assad has resisted for years.

Hezbollah is seeking an additional arena from where it can harm Israel, because conducting operations against the Jewish state from Lebanon is problematic, due to domestic political constraints (primarily fear of escalation and spillover effects on the Lebanese economy). Iran has a perennial interest in bleeding Israel. Creating a new threat from Syria serves this purpose. A new front in Syria will also enhance Iran's ability to deter an Israeli attack on its nuclear installations.

Israel's reaction

Deterrence can be enhanced, however, if Israel makes preparations for a large-scale operation against Hezbollah. This means building the necessary ground forces and training for Lebanese scenarios. Such a build-up process is not clearly evident so far, and Hezbollah might deduce that its huge arsenal (over 100,000 missiles) creates an effective deterrent. As the number of attacks on Israel from southern Lebanon has increased in recent months, the long period of quiet since 2006 seems more fragile. Perhaps Hezbollah is less afraid to hit Israeli targets. Deterrence against highly motivated rivals such as Hezbollah is always temporary and wears off with time. Israeli restraint is not conducive to restoration of deterrence. Therefore, the capability to destroy the Hezbollah missile threat is needed for deterring this radical organization, but also in case Israel finds it necessary to address such a threat before it attacks the Iranian nuclear infrastructure.

The attempts to change the security equation in the north call for a reassessment of Israel's policies toward Assad. If he is no longer able to resist the desire of Iran and Hezbollah to perpetrate terrorist acts against Israel from beyond the Golan Heights, his usefulness for Israel becomes limited. It is true that the civil war in Syria, where bad guys fight bad guys, is a convenient strategic development. Moreover, Israel (among other actors) has very limited influence on the outcome of the bloody struggle, but the survival of the Assad regime should no longer be a factor in Israel's strategic calculations.

If Assad falls

Actually, the fall of the Assad regime is nowadays in Israeli interest. The demise of this regime would be a terrible blow to its regional allies – Iran and Hezbollah. Damascus, an old ally of Tehran, is the linchpin of the Shiite crescent. And Iran is the most dangerous enemy of Israel and the main source for regional instability. The fall of Assad would also weaken Hezbollah considerably. It would reduce Hezbollah-Iranian influence in Lebanon and make the Hezbollah military build-up a more complicated enterprise. A Hezbollah without Iranian control of Damascus might spare Israel the need to intervene militarily in Lebanon in order to deal with the missile threat.

If Assad falls, it is not clear what will happen in Syria, but it is certain that Sunni radical groups will be more influential and the struggle over controlling parts of the country will continue. However, sub-state groups are generally less of a security threat than states. Assad-led Syria still has a chemical weapons arsenal and there are reports that it is trying to revive its nuclear weapons program.

An Israeli predisposition to discard Assad is also useful in Jerusalem's relations with Saudi Arabia, which loathes the Assad regime and understands that its fall will curtail the growing Iranian influence in the Middle East. It is the Iranian threat that constitutes the strategic glue between the two states.

The future ahead

In the near future, Israel is unlikely to be threatened by conventional armies in the region. Instead, Israel faces the threat of non-state entities motivated by Islamic ideology that have managed to amass increasing power and weaponry; Hezbollah, Hamas, the Islamic State and its offshoots. However, more dangerous is the possibility that some time in 2015, Iran will reach a deal with the West that will allow it to continue to pursue nuclear military capabilities. Israel's military must therefore be prepared for both ground warfare against Islamist extremists and an operation in Iran.

When summarizing the security situation in the State of Israel, no "real" army is among the threats that Israel faces in 2015. Some states still possess armies in the region, primarily Egypt, yet Israel does not seem to be their commanders' prime target. Egypt's military leaders have yet to cement their hold in Egypt itself, and they definitely have not found a way to solve its problems.

The rest of the militaries in the region are irrelevant for many reasons. The Syrian army is wasting strength fighting against Syrian civilians, and while it still possesses a substantial arsenal, its units have been compromised, its morale is extremely low, and many of its commanders fear for their lives if the other side should win.

The once-enormous Iraqi army, at one time seen as having the ability to change the balance of power on the eastern front against Israel, has ceased to exist. Today, the Americans are working to rebuild it, in the hopes that Iraq can assist them in the fight against the Islamic State.

The small but professional Jordanian army is looking east and north, toward the crumbling states of Iraq and Syria. Islamist terrorists are thriving within the power vacuum in both countries, and Jordan may already be in their crosshairs. Radical Islam could, potentially, rear its head in Jordan, and Amman certainly does not see Israel as an enemy. The Lebanese army was and remains a small force that is currently busy fending off Islamist extremists that are trying to export the war from Syria to tiny Lebanon, so far with little success.

While it is true that Saudi Arabia and the Persian Gulf emirates are arming themselves with the best Western weapons, mostly American ones, Israel is not their target. Iran, the dark cloud looming over the Persian Gulf, is the reason for the rapid arms race in that region. It is obvious that from the moment the weapons are there, anyone who is in control of those countries can use them. There is room for concern about the future, but that will require a great change that, if it should take place, will take a great deal of time.

After having been accustomed to a situation in which large regular armies with armor, artillery, hundreds of aircraft and thousands of troops were arrayed on Israel's borders, there can be no doubt that Israel has moved into a different world.

The current threat to Israel is different. It consists mainly of non-state entities motivated by Islamic ideology. The strongest of them is Hezbollah, which was formed with a dual purpose in mind: It represents Iran's long reach in the area and against Israel, while at the same time it aims to control Lebanon, where the Shiites are the largest ethnic group.

Hezbollah's capabilities most closely resemble those of an army. Its arsenal numbers some 150,000 missiles and rockets, several thousand of which have a range that cover the entire State of Israel. This rare and substantial firepower apparently even exceeded the firepower possessed by most of the European states combined.

Hezbollah also has long-range surface-to-sea missiles, anti-aircraft missiles, unmanned aerial vehicles, and modern anti-tank missiles. It is well organized into a military-style hierarchy and appears to possess command and control systems of high quality. It was established by Iranian leaders, but its leadership has always consisted of Lebanese people who were closely linked to Iran's interests. Hezbollah assisted the Shiites by providing for their needs in the civilian sphere as a base for building its military power.

Hezbollah is currently busy assisting Syrian President Bashar Assad's regime in Syria. It has sacrificed hundreds of its own people there and is acquiring substantial battle experience, but from its perspective, the battle is over its survival. It fights beside the Syrian Alawites because it needs them to stay in power. If Assad survives, Hezbollah's status in Lebanon will increase, as will its status in Damascus.

The second organization that constitutes a steadily rising threat to Israel is Hamas, which rules the Gaza Strip, where the group has established impressive military capabilities with assistance from Iran and Hezbollah. Its most significant capabilities are its ability to produce its own long-range rockets and its expanding grid of terror tunnels.

After Operation "Protective Edge" in Gaza, Hamas was left in possession of 3,500 rockets. The big question is the speed at which Hamas can regain the capabilities it has lost. For Hamas, the current regime in Egypt is a formidable obstacle. Hamas has the markings of a well-organized military organization, as well as an impressive ability to learn and improve.

The Islamic Jihad, largely run and established by Iran, operates alongside Hamas. Although the Islamic Jihad is a small organization with a smaller rocket arsenal of lower quality, it cannot be disregarded as insignificant.

Assuming that the current situation in Judea and Samaria continues as is, it does not appear that the security in the region will significantly decline. A deterioration in relations with the Palestinian Authority could lead to tension on the ground, mainly demonstrations and rioting and perhaps more grass-roots terrorism, but we can assume that this will be more of a policing challenge than a substantial security threat.

The most significant threat to Israel's very existence is the possibility that some time in 2015, Iran will reach a deal with the West that would allow it to pursue some form of nuclear military capability. This process will not come to fruition this year, but a bad deal with the superpowers would be an important milestone for Tehran.

This may be Israel's main security challenge, and any deal between Iran and the West will make it difficult for Israel to deal with it. This means that together with providing ongoing security, the Israeli military must be prepared for both large-scale ground warfare in Lebanon, attrition in Gaza and an operation in Iran – a feat that will be neither easy nor cheap

Hamas warfare

Since 2007, when Hamas gained control of the Gaza Strip, Gaza police and internal security forces and the Hamas military (the Qassam Brigades) have fallen under a joint command headed by Ahmed Jaabari. This allowed a unification of forces and established more effective command of Hamas' military capability. Once unified, Hamas began to focus on a military buildup in Gaza.

The focus shifted toward acquisition of advanced weapon systems such as longer-range rockets (from Iran), advanced anti-tank guided missiles (ATGMs) and increasingly powerful improvised explosive devices (IEDs). Yet, despite this unification of effort and focus on advanced systems, in 2008 the Israeli Defense Force (IDF) stated that it would "take a number of years" before the full effects of this build up would be felt. The coming conflict with Israel would prove this to be true.

The Qassam Brigades are the primary military organization operating in Gaza, but are not alone. In addition to Hamas, the Palestinian Islamic Jihad (PIJ) (more than 1,000 fighters) and the Popular Resistance Committee (PRC) (a few hundred fighters) are active in Gaza and at times work directly with Hamas.

Both groups have targeted Israel with rocket and mortar fire. Though estimates vary, the strength of the Qassam Brigades is believed to be between 6,000-10,000 fighters and thousands of part-time fighters— bringing the total potential fighting force to as many as 20,000. However, only a few hundred can be categorized as highly proficient Hamas fighters and leaders. Most of this latter group has participated in training in Syria and Iran and/or with Hezbollah in Lebanon.

Hamas divides Gaza into four operational sectors: northern (primary launch site for rockets), central, Gaza City and southern. Typical Hamas tactical actions have included suicide bombings, indirect rocket and mortar fire, small arms fire, ambushes, raids to destroy positions or abduct personnel, use of IEDs, surface-to-air fire (SAFIRE). They also have a highly competent internet presence and information operations (IO) capability.

Hamas is reported to have the following weapons: various Russian, US and Israeli small-arms and sniper rifles, grenades, ATGMs, rocket-propelled grenades (RPGs), IEDs, large amounts of explosives, various mortar and rockets (ranging from homemade Qassams to the more advanced long-range 122-mm Katyusha rockets acquired from Iran). Hamas has reportedly obtained *"air defense missiles and weapons—including the SA-7 and HN-5, and RPG-29s and possibly anti-tank guided missiles . . . from Iran, Syria, and the Hezbollah."*

In addition, Hamas used an extensive network of tunnels, IEDs, and a *"spider web of prepared strong points, underground hidden shelters, and ambush points throughout urban and built up areas as defensive strong points"* in the preparation of a fight with Israel. Weapons, money and fighters originating in Iran and Syria are also smuggled into the Gaza Strip through this network.

Israeli intelligence estimates that *"some 250 tons of explosives, 80 tons of fertilizer, 4,000 rocket-propelled grenades, and 1,800 rockets were transported from Egypt to Gaza from September 2005 to December 2008."*

This arms smuggling network is directed by Hamas and aided by the Iranian Islamic Revolutionary Guard Corps (IRGC). Yet, given all of this, Hamas does not appear to have a group of battle-tested fighters.

According to the Center for Strategic and International Studies, *"unlike Hezbollah, Hamas never had to develop the combat skills necessary to fight an effective opponent."* Much of Hezbollah's combat skills can be attributed to the existence of established Hezbollah training sites in Lebanon—staffed by foreigners, most notably IRGC advisors and trainers. Geographically, the crowded Gaza Strip does not afford such training opportunities.

Like Hezbollah, Hamas has effectively used rockets and mortars to attack and harass Israeli cities. During both the conflicts, Israel was unable to stop the rocket attacks. Yet, in terms of military power, Hamas simply lacks the combat power and effectiveness of Hezbollah. Hamas' military training is not as advanced as that provided to Hezbollah forces, nor does Hamas receive the most advanced weapons from its sponsors. Hamas generally lacks the sophistication of Hezbollah, and has proven more susceptible to Israeli targeting.

Hezbollah warfare

Hezbollah's Strategic Provenance

Hezbollah evolved as a state-sponsored, distinctly anti-Israeli organization—first as a military instrument of Syria, and then as Iran's strategic asset. When the Palestine Liberation Organization (PLO) was expelled from Jordan in 1975, it moved into Lebanon and spurred the growing Muslim majority to challenge the Maronite Christian government. The Muslim-Christian civil war ensued. Damascus exploited the resulting instability to take military control of Lebanon—which Syria considered its territory—in the hope of threatening Israel on its northern border and retaking the Golan Heights.

Supporting the Christian government, Israel intervened with air attacks in 1976 and, in March 1978, invaded Lebanon to provide a more effective deterrent. Shortly thereafter, Israel withdrew. After four more years of cross-border hostilities, Israel invaded again, this time with some 80,000 troops. Israel quickly routed the PLO and Syrian troops in the southern part of the country, and maintained its presence to deter further PLO and Syrian attacks. In 1983, Hezbollah arose as an anti-Israeli splinter group of Amal, an existing Shi'ite organization. Unable to confront Israel militarily, Syria nurtured Hezbollah, which became the most effective military force against Israel in Lebanon.

Simultaneously, the Shi'ite population was growing. According to estimates—hotly disputed among non-Shi'ite Lebanese parties—Shi'ites constituted 40 percent of Lebanon's population by the late 1990s. Hezbollah increasingly drew the support of Iran, Syria's ally, which enlisted the group as its militant Shi'ite and anti-Israeli proxy in the Arab world. Hezbollah's military effectiveness in drawing Israeli blood eventually afforded it political domination of South Beirut and south Lebanon.

Hezbollah enhanced its appeal by refraining from fighting other Lebanese factions during the civil war, by its incorruptibility, and through charity and community involvement. The organization became the leading proponent of an Islamic republic in Lebanon. As a consequence, despite growing domestic opposition to Hezbollah's armed status, some members of Hezbollah still consider armed hostility toward a common foe—Israel—the linchpin of Lebanon's security, if not its *raison d'être*.

Hezbollah characterizes Israel's 2000 strategic withdrawal from south Lebanon as a defeat at Hezbollah's hands. Hezbollah Deputy Secretary General Naim Qassem proclaimed: *"We do not need reassurances from anyone on behalf of Israel. What reassures us are our arms, our preparedness, and our readiness, and if Israel is planning any action, it knows the level of the response. This is what reassures us and nothing else."*

Hezbollah's core comprises several thousand activists, but, as evidenced by its political success, its broader popular support is orders of magnitude higher. Its highest governing body is the 17-member Majlis al-Shura, or Consultative Council, which since 1992 has been led by Secretary-General Hassan Nasrallah. Nasrallah made his revolutionary bones as a Hezbollah guerrilla commander in the 1980s; his religious education and personal charisma elevated him to overall leadership.

Nasrallah is also chairman of the Jihad Council, the organization's military decision-making body, which is one step below the Consultative Council in the organizational hierarchy. Hezbollah's organizational structure is essentially top-down, and its political and military dimensions are unified both structurally and in the person of Nasrallah. Accordingly, Hezbollah is not especially susceptible to deep splits along strategic or tactical lines. The Consultative Council also has formal links to Iran's Supreme Leader (currently Ayatollah Ali Khamenei) and informal ties to the elite Iranian Revolutionary Guards Corps (IRGC).

Hezbollah's domestic political legitimacy, however, rests not only on its Iranian and Syrian connections and its coercive power in the region, but also on its benevolent presence in Lebanon. While generally corrupt and dysfunctional Lebanese governments have been ineffectual welfare providers for decades, an efficient, incorruptible Hezbollah has furnished schools, medical assistance, and food for Lebanese people—mainly Shi'ites—in need.

Although Iran initially subsidized Hezbollah's welfare operations, since the 1990s it has consolidated a domestic support base, placing Hezbollah-flagged charity boxes, depicting cupped hands, in public areas throughout southern Lebanon. If the United States is to launch an effective initiative for demilitarization, it will need to make a compelling case to Hezbollah's constituency as well as the more pragmatic members of its leadership. Even for such improbable efforts, there is hopeful precedent.

Over the past few years, Israel and Hezbollah have both worked to improve their capabilities for the kind of war they expect to fight. And Syria's civil war has changed the strategic landscape greatly.

For its part, Hezbollah has massively expanded the size and range of its rocket and missile inventory. In 2006, it went to war with some 13,000 short- and medium-range rockets, allowing it to strike targets throughout northern Israel. Today it could have over 100,000 rockets and missiles, including a number of long-range systems as well as systems with improved accuracy, allowing it to strike throughout Israel and with increased precision.

Hezbollah is also believed to have made other improvements in its capabilities, including air defense and coastal defense, with systems acquired from or through Syria. It has very likely deepened and improved its anti-armor capabilities with additional anti-tank weapons. And it has improved its defensive layout in southern Lebanon, deeply embedding its offensive and defensive forces in various towns. In addition, the group claims to have developed a capability to undertake offensive ground operations into Israel. According to the director of production for Israeli military intelligence, Hezbollah forces may well penetrate the border and fight within northern Israel in the event of another war.

On January 27 2015, Hezbollah killed two Israeli soldiers in retaliation for the January 18 airstrike against its operatives in Syria, raising the potential for serious conflict to its highest level since the 2006 war. Although both sides are signaling that they are not interested in further escalation at the moment, future exchanges could rapidly devolve into all-out fighting. Furthermore, it is unclear whether Iran -- which lost a prominent general in last week's Israeli strike -- views Hezbollah's response as adequate, and it may yet prod the group toward further action.

Hezbollah's strategic situation has also changed following its commitment of significant forces to Syria, with an estimated 5,000 personnel serving there at any one time. On the one hand, this situation may dilute Hezbollah's interest in serious conflict with Israel, since it limits the number of forces the group could bring to bear. On the other hand, Hezbollah does not appear to have committed the kinds of forces (rocket/missile and antitank) that would be most useful against Israel, and it has gained operational experience in Syria that could make it more effective in a ground war. Moreover, the group could attempt to exploit its new situation by operating through Syrian territory on Israel's Golan front.

The Israel Defense forces have improved their capabilities dramatically since 2006 as well, including enhanced intelligence and strike firepower (air and artillery) that increase their ability to locate and hit targets. They have also enhanced their ground maneuver capabilities by deploying more advanced and capable tanks and armored personnel carriers (the Merkava IV and Namer, respectively) and equipping key armored units with the Trophy self-protection system, which can intercept antitank munitions. Since 2006, IDF ground training has emphasized operations against Hezbollah, though it is unclear how much of this has been done for reserve units.

Israel's ability to defend against Hezbollah's short-to-medium-range rocket threat has also been enhanced through deployment of the Iron Dome system, which did not exist in 2006. And its civil defense system has been upgraded and tested in recent conflicts with Hamas.

In addition to the unique tensions and triggers inherent in the Israel-Hezbollah situation, there are general military advantages to moving up the escalation ladder faster than one's opponent. Doing so allows one to seize the initiative, dictate a conflict's pace and scope, and execute one's plans with fewer restrictions. There is definitely an advantage to being "first with the most." Other factors that could lead to full-scale escalation include the snowballing of violence as each side ups its commitment, an incident that causes unexpected casualties, or domestic pressure to achieve victory.

Against these must be set certain brakes on escalation. For one, neither side can fully ignore its strategic situation, and neither seems eager to risk the extensive casualties and damage that all-out conflict could bring. Hezbollah's Syrian commitment makes it less capable of sustained conflict with Israel, and pressure from allies could steer both parties away from escalation. Whether or not these brakes would be enough to prevent war remains to be seen.

In the event of another large-scale fight, Hezbollah could conduct major offensive and defensive operations. Offensively, the centerpiece of its strategy could be a rocket and missile offensive throughout the depth of Israel. According to Israeli intelligence estimates, Hezbollah would likely attempt to sustain fire of around a thousand rockets and missiles per day, dwarfing the approximate daily rate of 118 achieved in 2006. Perhaps more important,

Hezbollah now has missiles with the range and accuracy to strike large strategic targets such as airfields, headquarters, and economically important sites.

An operation of this nature could overwhelm Israel's anti-rocket systems. The weight of the attack would fall on northern and to a lesser extent central Israel, but Hezbollah can now reach targets in the south as well.

The group could also attempt to penetrate Israel via Lebanon or Syria. As mentioned above, Hezbollah has threatened to do so in a future conflict, Israeli intelligence has acknowledged the threat, and the group's operations in Syria have probably given it a better capability to do so. In addition, last year's Gaza war highlighted the threat of offensive cross-border tunneling. While conditions on the Lebanon border are not as suitable for that tactic, Israel is concerned about it and actively searches for tunnels there.

Defensively, Hezbollah would attempt to limit the effectiveness of expected Israeli air operations by dispersing its forces into civilian areas and/or underground, and by using whatever antiaircraft weapons it has, perhaps including new or improved types of surface-to-air missiles. It would also try to blunt any Israeli ground advance into southern Lebanon by relying on its fortified localities there and using antitank and indirect fire systems.

On the other side, Israel could carry out two major offensive operations: An air operation against Hezbollah's rocket/missile forces and infrastructure throughout Lebanon. A large-scale, deep ground operation in which multiple divisions attack the group's ground and rocket/missile forces in southern Lebanon. The inability of airpower alone to negate the enhanced rocket/missile threat would likely make ground operations of some sort necessary.

Defensively, Israel would attempt to use active (Iron Dome and Patriot batteries) and passive (civil defense) measures to reduce the effects of Hezbollah's rocket/missile offensive while waiting for IDF offensive operations to diminish the threat. This would likely mean destroying launch forces throughout Lebanon and seizing launch areas in southern Lebanon. Israel would also have to be prepared to fight on its own soil in the event of a successful penetration.

A general conflict could be expected to produce significant military and civilian casualties on both sides. Fighting on the ground in southern Lebanon and perhaps northern Israel would likely produce the most military casualties. And if civilians were present amid ground operations -- a likelihood in southern Lebanon -- they would suffer significant casualties in those areas. Civilian casualties should also be expected in areas where air and rocket/missile strikes are conducted, especially when defense measures are inadequate.

Damage to civil infrastructure can be expected in both Israel and Lebanon. If Hezbollah can sustain high rates of fire on Israel, some weapons will get through and some targets will be struck, whether through sheer numbers or greater accuracy. And since Hezbollah operates from within civilian areas, Israeli strikes would cause some damage there even when precautions and precision tactics are employed. Lebanese infrastructure such as bridges, roads, and communications facilities would also be targeted because of their military utility.

Such a war would likely cause widespread social and economic disruption in Israel and Lebanon. Hamas was able to achieve this in southern Israel last year, and attacks further north showed the potential for countrywide disruption under sustained rocket fire. Similarly, the 2006 war demonstrated that Israeli air operations could reach deep into Lebanon with significant economic and social impact. A new war would likely bring more widespread air attacks with even broader effects.

Accepting that Hezbollah, like Hamas, cannot be destroyed by military action alone, Israel would likely focus on achieving limited but clear strategic objectives in a new war, such as substantially reducing the group's military capabilities and damaging enough infrastructure to sully its reputation as defender of Lebanon, perhaps increasing public antagonism toward it in the process.

Of course, critics within and outside Israel would protest these objectives for various reasons. And an extended conflict with significant casualties could increase pressure to expand the mission. A major conflict with Hezbollah could also complicate Israel's relations with the United States. If Israel initiates large-scale operations, Obama administration sources might call for restraint, perhaps even painting the action as an effort to collapse the Iranian nuclear negotiations.

A major conflict would also have important implications for the Syria war. Fighting could spread into Syria along the Golan frontier and bring Assad regime forces under Israeli fire. Hezbollah could also be forced to withdraw troops from Syria in order to meet an Israeli offensive in southern Lebanon, weakening the critical support it has provided to Damascus. And if the group suffers major military losses to Israel, its long-term ability to lend such support could be compromised.

Current expectations that Israel and Hezbollah can manage escalation may or may not hold true; similar assessments were made before all of the recent Gaza conflicts (2009, 2012, 2014), and Hezbollah's drastic miscalculation sparked the 2006 war. If a new conflict does in fact break out, Israel and Lebanon are in for a very difficult time. War in 2015 would probably be significantly more intense and destructive than in 2006, and all of Israel would likely be targeted, not just the north. Such a conflict would bring significant pressure to achieve a clear success, further driving the parties to sustain the fighting and raise it to higher levels of violence.

According to Brigadier General Itay Baron, head of the IDF Military Intelligence research section, Hezbollah now has around 65,000 rockets and missiles, many times the number they had on the eve of the 2006 war. Particularly worrisome is the Tishreen missile, which contains control and guidance systems that have given Hezbollah a precision-strike capability.

The group also possesses Iranian-made rockets such as the Fajr-3 and Fajr-5, with respective ranges of 27 and 45 miles; and a huge quantity of simpler 107mm and 122mm rockets with ranges up to 12 miles. These rockets are capable of striking many cities in northern Israel, such as Haifa, Tiberias, Afula, Nahariya, and Safed. Hezbollah intends to use them in order to paralyze life in Israel through intense barrages of rocket and missile fire; something Hezbollah proved itself quite capable of doing already in 2006.

Hezbollah has also upgraded its anti-aircraft missiles, anti-ship cruise missiles, anti-tank missiles, and reconnaissance and attack drones; all of which would make Israeli retaliatory strikes far more difficult. The group notoriously displayed its anti-ship capabilities in 2006 by firing a Noor anti-ship missile at the Israeli naval vessel INS *Hanit*. It may now have obtained Russian Yakhont anti-ship cruise missiles from Syria.

If these weapons have indeed been transferred to Hezbollah, it would instantly put any Israeli naval vessel under direct threat, even those docked at Israeli ports. The Yakhont is difficult to defend against, since it can be launched from beyond the horizon, at supersonic speeds and with a range of different possible trajectories. If fired from behind mountain ridges or other geographical obstacles in Lebanon, they could avoid detection from the sea and strike targeted vessels with minimal warning. It is believed that 12 of these missiles may be in the hands of Hezbollah fighters in Syria itself.

Israeli military officials are now beginning to view the Hezbollah threat as strategic rather than tactical; that is, they are preparing for a confrontation with a foreign army, rather than a terrorist group. But this army is not like others, because while it has the size and capacity of an army, it still fights like a "terrorist" organization. The tactics it has adopted would pose a growing challenge to any military, even one as experienced in asymmetric operations as the IDF.

Hezbollah's combat tactics have been increasingly refined over recent years, and the group is now on the cutting edge of terrorist and jihadi warfare. It has gained substantial combat experience from its battles with Israel and especially with Syrian rebel forces, as well as sharing tactical knowledge with other jihadist groups around the world.

The organization's style of fighting is based, generally speaking, on guerilla and jihadi tactics. Due to the asymmetrical nature of combat between terrorist organizations and state military forces, groups like Hezbollah have adopted what are called "counter-value strategies," which target civilians and civilian infrastructure. This is distinguished from traditional "counter-force strategies," which target military infrastructure. This makes such groups extremely difficult to fight, especially for armies like the IDF that go to great lengths to protect civilian lives on both sides. Hezbollah is an acknowledged master of counter-value strategy, and serves as a role model for groups like Hamas, which is adopting similar tactics.

Hezbollah possesses a sophisticated weapons arsenal as well as military capabilities beyond anything Israel can even start to comprehend, the Shiite terror group's chief claimed

"The resistance in Lebanon has everything the enemy can imagine and not imagine," Hassan Nasrallah said during an interview with Lebanese television station Al Mayadeen. "We have weapons of all types, whatever comes to mind," the Hezbollah leader added, according to the Lebanese Daily Star news site.

Nasrallah further stated that should Israel choose to provoke his organization, Hezbollah was fully prepared for a military confrontation with the Jewish state. *"If Israel attacks Lebanon, our resistance is strong and our ability to win is great,"* he said.

According to a statement by Al Mayadeen, Nasrallah also addressed reports that a senior official in the Lebanese terror group's external operations unit named Mohammad Shorbah was facing trail for treason after allegedly assisting Israel's Mossad spy agency.

Lebanon's security agencies periodically report the exposure of Israeli-recruited agents in the country, as well as of listening devices planted in the south of the country.

Hezbollah was first alerted to the possibility of a foreign agent in its ranks in the aftermath of a bus bombing in the Bulgarian resort town of Burgas in 2012 that killed five Israeli tourists and a local bus driver, a report in the Daily Star said, citing an anonymous security source.

The group's suspicion was reportedly aroused when the Bulgarian interior minister accused it of being behind the attack. Shorbah had informed Israel that Hezbollah was behind the attack, and Jerusalem, in turn, relayed the information to the Bulgarian authorities.

Shorbah, who also allegedly played a key role in the 2008 assassination of top Hezbollah official Imad Mughniyeh in Damascus, thwarted five attempts by the group to avenge his death, piquing Hezbollah's suspicions in the process.

Mughniyeh's assassination was considered a major blow to the group, and while Israel never claimed responsibility, Hezbollah has blamed Jerusalem for the attack. There has been no official reaction from Israel on the reports.

A senior IDF official warned that while Hezbollah has no immediate plan to attack Israel, a minor security incident could erupt into a full-fledged war on Israel's northern front during which the terror organization would likely try to capture swaths of the Galilee.

Hezbollah has managed a number of cross-border attacks on Israel, sometimes placing explosives next to army infrastructure. In 2006, the group killed two soldiers and nabbed their bodies, sparking a bloody war.

Speaking in an interview with Iran's Fars News Agency, Commander of the IRGC's Aerospace Force, Brig-Gen. Amir Ali Hajizadeh said, "*Based on our information, Hezbollah's power has so much increased in recent years that they can attack any target in any part of the occupied territories with a high precision capability and with a very low margin of error.*"

Hajizadeh added that Hezbollah "*has always shown that its actions in the battlefield are unexpected and it showed this capability well during the 33-day war (against Israel in summer 2006) and it can make similar moves on any scene today.*"

The IRGC's website quoted Hajizadeh as saying that Hassan al-Laqqis, the Hezbollah military commander assassinated in Beirut, played a major role in increasing the organizations strike capabilities. Israel has flatly denied Hezbollah claims that it was behind the assassination of Laqqis. Laqqis, who is believed to have commanded Hezbollah troops fighting in Syria's civil war, was shot in the head from close range outside his home in the Hadath district of the Lebanese capital on December 4, 2013. Hezbollah leader Hassan Nasrallah vowed to exact revenge on Israel for the killing of Laqqis.

A RAND study concludes that overall "*Hezbollah retains a stronger, more capable, fighting force. While Hamas primarily operates as a traditional insurgency group, Hezbollah can manifest both insurgent-like skills and more-conventional operational and tactical skills.*"

Hezbollah's military wing, the Islamic Resistance (IR), can be divided into two types of fighters: the so-called "elite," or core fighters—numbering between 300 and 1,000 (*perhaps as many as 3,000*) and local fighters that can be called to action as needed. The number of local fighters cannot be accurately estimated, because they often include many not formally associated with Hezbollah, but the number may be as high as 10,000. Both Hamas and Hezbollah claim the ability to easily increase its fighting force size—by relying on the willingness of the local population to join the fight.

Hezbollah organizes its fighters into small, self-sufficient teams capable of operating independently and without direction from higher authority for long periods of time. The most significant aspect of Hezbollah's organization is the high degree of autonomy given to junior leaders. This is a function of Iranian doctrinal influences and the entrepreneurial nature of Lebanese society.

Hezbollah's weapons inventory includes massive amounts of artillery rockets (Zelzal-2, the Nazeat, the Fajr-3 and -5, 302-mm, 220-mm, 122-mm, 107-mm); ATGMs (ranging from the AT-14, AT-5, AT-13 METIS-M, AT-3, AT-4, Milan, TOW, RPG-29 and the RPG-7); surface-to-air missiles; and anti-ship missiles.

Hezbollah also posses an unmanned aerial vehicle (UAV) fleet, including 30 Mirsad-1 UAVs from Iran, that gives it an impressive long-range sensor-to-shooter link. Exact numbers are hard to ascertain, but sources believe that Hezbollah has replenished much of pre-2006 munitions inventory since the end of the latest conflict with Israel. The best-known weapon in Hezbollah's inventory is the Katushya rocket, some models of which have a range of 45 miles that has been used repeatedly against Israel.

Prewar estimates indicated that Hezbollah had accumulated up to 12,000 munitions, the vast majority of which were the Katushya. The rockets are notoriously inaccurate, but they served as an area-effect weapon intended to terrorize Israeli citizens and taunt the Israeli military, demonstrating the myth of Israel's military invincibility—Israel's prime strategic asset. Hezbollah enjoys a wider range of weapons than Hamas, notably in terms of more anti-tank weapons, and UAVs.

Both Hamas and Hezbollah are the foremost practitioners and adherents to the military doctrine of Muqawama, or resistance. This doctrine is based on an *"ideological view according to which Israel is particularly unable and unwilling to absorb causalities and make sacrifices."*

Put simply a war of attrition favors the insurgent Islamists. Unlike Hamas, Hezbollah's recent actions against Israel showed it to be an effective fighting force on many levels. Hezbollah remains the only Arab or Muslim entity to successfully face the Israelis in combat and this provides them with tremendous military cachet.

Hezbollah Demilitarized?

Some of Hezbollah's Lebanese opponents have greeted any suggestion of comparability between the IRA and Hezbollah with a skepticism verging on derision. They correctly point out that whereas the IRA enjoyed no direct and focused state support for terrorist operations and the UK strategically had nothing to fear from the Republic of Ireland, Hezbollah is merely the near enemy, and Iran the more potent far enemy, of Lebanon.

Unless the Iranian tree is weakened, they argue, the Hezbollah branch will remain largely intact. Moreover, they contend that notwithstanding superficial appearances to the contrary, Hezbollah is not being Lebanonized but rather vice-versa: Hezbollah is politically and militarily co-opting the Lebanese state so that it can serve as a platform for destroying Israel, which is Hezbollah's ultimate goal. The fear of some Lebanese is that Hezbollah is in fact quite happy to sacrifice Lebanon on the altar of its obsession with Israel.

While this view is understandable given Hezbollah's violent proclivities and maximalist rhetoric, it is almost certainly hyperbolic. Hezbollah leaders maintain stringent control over official pronouncements, and statements from Hezbollah figures diverging from its overarching message of defiance are rare.

Yet there are signs that Hezbollah has lost some legitimacy among its followers—and knows it. First, by turning its weapons on fellow Lebanese in May 2008 over the government's attempt to dismantle its covert communications network, Hezbollah breached a standing promise.

In May 2009, for instance, Hezbollah had meetings with both International Monetary Fund and European Union officials to discuss outside financial support for Lebanon. Last December, Nasrallah himself gave a speech urging adherence to Lebanese law—including paying for government water and electricity, abiding by building laws and civil codes, ending smuggling that hurts Lebanese business, and exhorting civil servants to perform their duties.

In the same time frame, of course, he also spoke of continued resistance to Israel and "the next war." But this dissonant message reflects the political necessity of courting the Arab street, and, as Raad's expressed openness to further discussions with the British suggests, does not preclude the discreet exploration of eventual demilitarization.

While the Hezbollah bloc did retain strong support against the Western-backed Sunni Muslim, Christian, and Druze coalition in Lebanon's June 2009 elections, taking 57 of 128 parliamentary seats, this performance did not reflect a surge in legitimacy. Thus, there may be a marginally greater incentive than is generally thought for Hezbollah to loosen its attachment to its weapons.

Indeed, it often appears that Hezbollah's new priority, like the IRA's 15 years ago, is to move more decisively into the political domain. The recent RAND study concludes that *"Hezbollah's behavior is...informed by questions of domestic legitimacy; it has recently taken great pains to publicly distance itself from Iranian patronage."*

This is clearly an issue: In a January 25 opinion piece addressed to Hezbollahi Minister of State for Administrative Reform Mohammed Fneish in the Lebanese daily *Al-Akhbar*, Member of Parliament Hassan Khalil angrily attacked Hezbollah's use of its arsenal for political intimidation: *"Your fierceness will not scare us while your weapons wreak havoc in the land and while you impose a sectarian electoral law upon us, appoint your men in the functions of the state, run corrupted municipalities, and control the judiciary and security forces. Your weapons terrorize us."* Khalil also implored Hezbollah to forswear the implicit backing of Damascus and Tehran and leave the use of force in Lebanon to the Lebanese state: *"Enough, rest, put your weapons down, and apologize."*

If Lebanon is to complete the long transition from a war-ravaged Syrian protectorate to something resembling the tolerant and workable polity it was before its civil war, the authority of its elected government will have to supplant Hezbollah as the prevailing source of order. This cannot occur without Hezbollah's effective demilitarization. And Hezbollah does have reasons to consider moving in that direction.

Syria's withdrawal from Lebanon, due to its suspected complicity in the assassination of former Lebanese Prime Minister Rafic Hariri in 2005, made it strategically weaker, while Damascus's subsequent willingness to participate in Turkish-brokered peace negotiations with Israel reflected Syrian President Bashar Al Assad's desire to establish common ground with Washington.

It is true that more recently Syria has re-asserted itself as Hezbollah's patron— for example, insisting that Lebanese politicians visiting Damascus be accompanied by a senior Hezbollah minder. Precisely because its presence in Lebanon is diminished, Syria is regionally more reliant on Hezbollah, while Hezbollah has strengthened its hand vis-à-vis Syria. The result is that their relationship has been further tightened. This does not necessarily mean the Hezbollah wants to be closer to Syria, only that it cannot comfortably spurn such a strong historical ally.

Hezbollah's very success in Lebanese politics and in the 2006 war with Israel has furnished it with sufficient confidence and bearing to move beyond its proxy relationship with Syria. Indeed, for some Hezbollah supporters, Syria has hampered Hezbollah by limiting its domestic political appeal to pro-Syria Lebanese. Whatever Assad's current disposition, Syria remains regionally weaker, and that fact may well have changed the Hezbollah leadership's calculations about Hezbollah's political legitimacy versus the retention of arms and posture of anti-Israeli resistance.

Certainly, Hezbollah still has substantial incentives for retaining its arsenal. While Israel's withdrawal from southern Lebanon a decade ago and Hezbollah's subsequent electoral success removed the immediate necessity for weapons as a matter of self-defense, for many powerful members of Hezbollah, armed hostility toward Israel remains the most persuasive and effective means of maintaining a privileged position in Lebanese politics.

Qassem also declared that *"had it not been for the heroic and brave fighters who invaded positions and killed Israeli soldiers to the point where the latter became afraid of even mentioning the name of Hezbollah, we would not have achieved victory and we could not have ousted Israel from this country with Allah's guidance and will."*

Furthermore, at the Doha conference in May 2008 aimed at ending conflict between government forces and Hezbollah militants, the Hezbollah-led opposition was accorded 11 of 30 cabinet seats—an effective veto over cabinet decisions, which require a two-thirds majority vote. To an extent, this confirmed Hezbollah's sustained strength in the non-violent political arena. Some Hezbollah leaders no doubt read the Doha compromise as a mandate for it to keep its weapons, not relinquish them. But others most likely do not.

Since the United States and its partners would pursue Hezbollah's demilitarization not to facilitate Hezbollah's quest to exploit the Lebanese state and society to advance its militant goals, but rather to establish a freer political marketplace that would induce Hezbollah to moderate its goals, hardline Hezbollah members would almost certainly oppose any movement in that direction. But other Hezbollah leaders might see measured cooperation in a demilitarization scheme as a new avenue for increasing its legitimacy and electoral appeal. Despite heavy resistance from some quarters (notably the notoriously defiant South Armagh Brigade), that is precisely the dynamic that took hold with the IRA in the early 1990s.

The goal, then, is to engage Hezbollah for the precise purpose of constraining it. How can this be done? It should start with appeals to Hezbollah's outside supporters. At the operational level, the first order of business would be to establish more effective control over Iranian weapons coming to Hezbollah across the Syrian border or into Lebanese ports and airfields. Iran, of course, has no disposition to roll itself back in the region, so direct pressure on Tehran would be fruitless. Syria, however, may be more amenable to cooperative overtures, depending on how they are framed.

On this score, the re-establishment of diplomatic relations between the United States and Syria and reports of upbeat meetings between U.S. Undersecretary of State William Burns and Syrian President Bashar Al Assad, and between State Department Counter-terrorism Coordinator Daniel Benjamin and his Syrian counterparts in mid-February, are provisionally positive signs. More substantively, in October 2009, shortly after U.S. troops confiscated eight containers of small-arms ammunition apparently bound for Hezbollah from the Hansa India, Syria reportedly held up a shipment of Iranian weapons to Hezbollah. This was apparently in response to Washington's wish for a demonstration of Syria's good faith.

In April, however, Israeli officials alleged that Syria had delivered long-distance Scud ballistic missiles to Hezbollah. While Hezbollah and Hariri himself have denied these accusations, and U.S. officials questioned them, Israeli commentators reasoned that Damascus had become pessimistic about the prospects for making a deal with Israel on the Golan Heights, and were opting instead to step up the pressure.

One lesson here is that absent a larger Israel-Syria peace accord, outright disarmament of Hezbollah—i.e., the destruction or custodial transfer of weapons—is infeasible. But that's not what the demilitarization initiative proposed here would involve. Even if Syria has in fact furnished Scuds to Hezbollah, its earlier restraint at the United States's behest shows that diplomacy can limit the importation of heavy weapons in the right circumstances. President Obama has indicated that his administration will make resuscitating prospects for Arab-Israeli accommodation a higher priority going forward. If that effort bears fruit, Syria may again become more willing to limit arms transfers.

Even with little or no Syrian cooperation, a reinforced UNIFIL II, aided by enhanced U.S. and Israeli technical surveillance, would hinder the flow of arms over the border if the Lebanese government consented to a broader UNIFIL II mandate and UNIFIL II contributors were willing to go along. Thus denying Hezbollah access to external weapons supplies—particularly the rockets that proved so provocative vis-A -vis Israel in 2006—would make it less capable of waging war, less inclined to do so, and probably more susceptible to a demilitarization arrangement involving its formidable existing arsenal if provided with Israeli and international assurances that it would not be attacked.

U.S. Calculations

An armed-and-dangerous Hezbollah clearly is not conducive to stable civil government. Hezbollah's 2006 war with Israel, which resulted from miscalculations by both sides, showed that large weapons stocks outside of the Lebanese government's control, in Hezbollah's hands, only undermine its authority and enrich the conditions for armed conflict. Reports in January of this year that Syria had allowed Hezbollah to use its territory to train in the use of advanced SA-2 surface-to-air missiles prompted warnings from U.S. officials that if Damascus supplied Hezbollah with such missiles, Israel would go to war with Syria. At the very least, as long as it is robustly armed, Hezbollah can indulge the temptation to dominate Lebanon through the threat of force, as it did in May 2008, raising the specter of civil war.

There is at least a limited opportunity for the United States to orchestrate change in Lebanon. Some observers have credited the "Obama effect" with the relative success of the pro-Western March 14 Alliance headed by Saad Hariri— named for the "Cedar Revolution" protests on March 14, 2005 triggered by his father's assassination—against Hezbollah in last June's Lebanese election. While it is unclear that it was in fact decisive, Hezbollah leaders may have made similar assessments. Lebanese who want to see their country normalized—and, therefore,

Hezbollah demilitarized—are perplexed and dismayed by Washington's apparent lack of interest in the issue and don't trust it to prioritize Lebanon's integrity over realpolitik concerns. After the 2006 war, one Lebanese man told journalist Michael Totten, "We love America, but have doubts. They let Syria come in here in 1991 for help in Iraq." The same man rued that "Hezbollah in

America is seen as terrorists, I know, but they are a large party in Lebanon and we have to live here with them." For good reason, Lebanese parties are thoroughly intimidated by Hezbollah, and will not push hard for its demilitarization until they are assured of strong and sustained American backing.

In any case, outside powers can no longer contain Hezbollah only by confronting its state supporters, but must also deal with the organization directly—especially if the objective is to shape the environment for eventual disarmament. It is hard to see how this can happen unless the United States follows up on the UK's foray. A diplomatic nod to Hezbollah would serve broader aims of U.S. Middle East policy—namely, rolling back Iranian influence in the region and establishing a regional coalition against Tehran, as well as securing a free and open Lebanon.

To accomplish these goals, it is essential that the United States compete with Iran for influence in Lebanon, and the only credible way to do that is to weigh in decisively in favor of a normalized Lebanese state through sustained, energetic diplomatic activity and an expressed willingness to facilitate demilitarization on the ground. Absent this high level of commitment, any approach to Hezbollah would be seen as mere acknowledgment of its political strength and leave its opposition feeling even more isolated and abandoned than before, and even less inclined to challenge Hezbollah's armed status.

Achieving a stable Lebanon insulated from internal disruption and external threat calls for overt diplomatic contact with Hezbollah in the framework of a policy aimed at eliminating Hezbollah's ability to press its agenda through force both within Lebanon and across the border into Israel. Obama is already committed to re-energizing a paralyzed Arab-Israeli process of reconciliation. Hezbollah's political and potential material support for Hamas significantly inhibits the process. A credible demilitarization framework might at least marginally lower Israel's perceptions of Hezbollah's threat and improve the presently bleak outlook for that process.

Without question, Washington has numerous disincentives to establishing any official contact with Hezbollah, which is, after all, a terrorist group among other things. Obama faces criticism at home for talking to Iran in the wake of the regime's domestic excesses; vitriolic rhetoric about Israel and the Holocaust and accompanying accusations of exposing Israel to a genocidally inclined adversary; and obvious Iranian duplicity on the nuclear issue. The

Administration's openness to a rapprochement with Syria is also subject to some doubts.

Scarcely a week after Burns met with Assad, the Syrian leader hosted Iranian President Mahmoud Ahmadinejad and Hezbollah's Nasrallah at a Damascus summit, and thus appeared unlikely to jettison old strategic relationships or to embrace new ones quickly. In addition, the Iraqi government—though apparently with little foundation—has attributed the bombings of the finance and foreign ministries in Baghdad to Syria. Some critics also consider Obama's opposition to Israel's settlements policy to constitute overreaching.

These factors would make any willingness on his part to approach Iran and Syria's most dangerous proxy against Israel open to vituperative debate. If Syria has indeed supplied Scuds to Hezbollah, resort to diplomacy would be greeted by even greater skepticism. Yet these circumstances also argue for bold action, outside the box, so as to break the patterns of internal intimidation and external provocation that have accompanied Hezbollah's political ascendance.

What the United States can do that other parties cannot do—not Saudi Arabia at Taif in 1989, not the UN after Hariri's assassination—is marshal broad domestic and international support for a demilitarization process. While Washington's tactical disincentives to doing so have been noted, it faces no insurmountable strategic barriers. Aside from logistical support for the bombing of the Khobar Towers in 1996 it is believed to have furnished, and suspected training of the Mahdi Army in Iraq several years ago, Hezbollah hasn't conducted hostile operations targeting the United States in a generation. Furthermore, Hezbollah leaders must worry that that Israel will again confront Hezbollah militarily—possibly very soon, other things being equal—in a more tactically measured and strategically sustainable manner, and therefore might conclude that talking about demilitarization would yield Hezbollah some temporary protection.

Nevertheless, given Hezbollah's lethal historical enmity toward the United States, and the reality that it does not crucially need American recognition or support, Washington would have to deal cautiously and circumspectly with Hezbollah. Here the American experience in Northern Ireland offers some qualified lessons. Discreet U.S. political support for Northern Irish nationalists helped solidify Sinn Fein's determination to pursue a non-violent political path. Domestically, President Clinton had to strike a delicate balance between enthusiastic Irish-American politicians and more skeptical players, including the law-enforcement and intelligence communities. Internationally, he had to control the risk of offending the British government and impairing the "special relationship."

The gambit paid off when the IRA announced its unilateral cease-fire in August 1994. Clinton then appointed a prestigious special representative, George Mitchell, to take the lead in framing and shepherding a self-consciously high-profile peace process and lent it political support by, among other things, personally visiting Belfast in November 1995. Granted, when the IRA broke its cease-fire less than three months later by bombing Canary Wharf, and it was revealed to have been planning the operation as Clinton toured Catholic West Belfast, the White House was angry and chagrined.

But Washington did not abandon its support for the peace process. After the IRA reinstated its cease-fire in July 1997, Mitchell's demonstrated even-handedness kept moderate unionists on board. He effectively mediated the multiparty talks that culminated in the Good Friday Agreement and the IRA's agreement in principle to demilitarize.

For Washington to hope for that kind of eventual result in Lebanon, it would have to prepare the ground with Congress as well as with Israel and interested Arab governments, thoroughly explaining its strategy and sequencing and securing cooperation and support. Just as Washington kept London and Dublin well apprised of its moves in Northern Ireland and discussed possible inducements with them, the U.S. government would have to keep the Israeli government and some Arab governments continually informed and broach with them any new security or political arrangements that might be conducive to peace.

In particular, to give Hezbollah's leaders maximum incentive to consider demilitarization, and insure itself as effectively as possible against the potential embarrassment of a Hezbollah backslide to violence, Washington should explore whether Israel would in principle agree to withdraw from the Shebaa Farms—the eight square-mile patch of land on the Lebanon-Syria border claimed by both governments—and refrain from attacking Lebanon in the event that Hezbollah agreed to some degree of demilitarization. The Israeli occupation has provided Hezbollah with a pretext for attacking the IDF and Syria with an excuse for deferring border negotiations with Lebanon.

Thus, an Israeli pullout would remove both a reason for Hezbollah to retain weapons and a source of Syrian diplomatic obstructionism. In addition, the Obama Administration would have to line up a major-power coalition to support and participate in a new and tough UNIFIL II mission, with a mandate to monitor and interdict cross-border arms traffic. At minimum, the UK, France, Germany, and probably Russia would have to back this initiative.

Bilaterally, U.S military assistance to Lebanon is a valuable carrot. The Bush Administration provided more than $300 million in tactical aid to the Lebanese Armed Forces (LAF) after the Syrian withdrawal in 2005, making Lebanon the second-largest per-capita recipient of U.S. military aid, after Israel. But Washington refrained from furnishing the sorts of strategic weapons—guided rockets, tanks, modern artillery, aircraft, and intelligence-gathering equipment—needed for a robust national defense.

The Obama Administration has essentially maintained the Bush team's position. In 2009, among the equipment the United States provided to the LAF were a dozen unmanned aerial vehicles, some inflatable boats, and a combat-support airplane—in other words, nothing close to real firepower. Such restraint is understandable given Hezbollah's power within Lebanon and the fear that potent weapons could fall into its hands.

Cobra attack helicopters had been tentatively discussed as part of the 2009 U.S. assistance package, but the prospect faded over worries that they would end up being used by Hezbollah. But American restraint on arms transfers also inadvertently strengthens Hezbollah's domestic case for holding on to its weapons by allowing Hezbollah to maintain that, without them, Lebanon's national defense would be insufficient. To dampen this rationale, American policymakers should link the quality and quantity of American assistance to the Lebanese army to strong Lebanese support for an international disarmament effort.

Strategic Communication

At the strategic level, lofty overtures have already been made. Various UNSC resolutions and international agreements, albeit with no current momentum behind them, mandate Hezbollah's disarmament.. The French have led the international charge for following through, and now the British have added their own bilateral efforts. Guarded American participation would make for a full, if largely ad hoc, effort from the three Western permanent members of the Security Council.

Even with that level of great-power backing, though, the idea of disarming Hezbollah still seems risible to many in the Middle East, including some of Hezbollah's once and perhaps future political rivals in Lebanon, such as Druze leader Walid Jumblatt and Free Patriotic Movement head Michel Aoun, both of whom are part of Hezbollah's coalition. But since the Cedar Revolution and the coalescence of the March 14 Alliance, more frequent and energized calls for Hezbollah's disarmament have been heard, especially from Maronite Christian leaders Amin Gemayel and Samir Geagea as well as Hariri. They do not, however, see themselves as strong enough singly or collectively to press the point.

The three powers must not only keep raising the subject of demilitarization within the Lebanese political system, but they also need to prevail on others to do so. Grand demarches notwithstanding, disarmament cannot happen unless public discourse in Lebanon demands it. Accordingly, to prepare the political ground in Lebanon for a major diplomatic initiative, the United States, the United Kingdom, and France will have to mount a concerted effort to convince Lebanese parliamentarians and journalists that they are committed to dealing with the issue of Hezbollah's arsenal and to reassure them that their support remains steadfast. The larger point is that great-power involvement needs to be ongoing and calibrated and not merely sporadic or crisis-driven.

Certainly a U.S. initiative to talk to Hezbollah would be a sensitive and controversial diplomatic effort. In fact, some Lebanese as well as American observers hold that, however imperfect, a relatively stable equilibrium now exists in Lebanon, and that casually considered attempts to change the political dispensation could end up producing disorder and potentially civil war.

To avoid this sort of blowback, the United States would have to acknowledge to Hezbollah that demilitarization could not proceed without Hezbollah's voluntary consent and participation. At the same time, Hezbollah itself would be more inclined to go along with a process involving quiet, negotiated demilitarization than one driven solely or mainly by magisterial pronouncements by outside powers.

Thus, sustained ground-level diplomatic contact would be necessary to give the effort the best chance of succeeding. Obviously, direct contact between senior

U.S. officials and, say, Nasrallah or Qassem would confer too much legitimacy on Hezbollah to be diplomatically feasible—even in the supremely unlikely event that such senior Hezbollah figures would agree to meet with Americans. An appropriate course of action would be for the State Department instead to dispatch mid-level U.S. officials to establish a link with Hezbollah representatives, or possibly for President Obama to appoint a special envoy for this purpose as President Clinton did with respect to Northern Ireland.

Either way, the diplomatic mandate would be to talk to all parties about disarmament and not to have an exclusive dialogue with Hezbollah. To attract the widest international support, however, the Administration should also carry out its approach to Hezbollah openly and unapologetically, and with determination and commitment.

The proposal here is for an elaborate, diplomatically and militarily complex initiative that would derive credibility and momentum from the sustained attention and leadership of the United States and other major powers. It would also expose Lebanese parties to potentially serious near-term risk. Is Lebanon's political integrity worth that risk?

From the moral and political perspective of the Lebanese people, who have still not recovered from an eviscerating civil war that began in 1975 and remain pawns of Iran, Syria, and Hezbollah, the answer must be yes. From the broader geopolitical perspective of the United States and its international partners, in which rolling back Iranian influence in the Middle East and shaping an environment more conducive to Arab-Israeli accommodation are crucial goals, the answer is an even more resounding yes.

IDF alarm

Lieutenant General Benny Gantz said that Hezbollah has become the seventh military power in the world, adding that only the US, Russia, France, Britain, China and 'Israel' possess more fire power than the party.

Speaking at the Herzliya Conference, Gantz pointed out that 'Israel' has to be worried about the military experiences which Hezbollah gained from its intervention in Syria, stressing that the Israeli army has to be alert at the northern borders because Hezbollah fighters still deploy in the area.

The Israeli military chief added that Hezbollah has fought in Syria at several fronts simultaneously, what threatens 'Israel' if the party accumulates and uses all these military capabilities to fight Israel. Gantz considered that the developments in Syria do not serve Israeli interests as long as President Assad rules that country. On Iran, Gantz claimed that using the military power to halt Tehran's nuclear program is "a must".

Israel's Chief of Staff Lieutenant-General Benny Gantz (L) flanked by Israeli Defense Minister Moshe Yaalon in a press conference at the Defence Ministry in Tel Aviv, on March 5, 2014": "*The bad news from our point of view, is that while Hezbollah is fighting on three fronts... it is also amassing experience which we will one day face,*" he added. Gantz warned that in Syria there is "*a radical axis developing, led by Iran and Hezbollah. The Lebanese terror organization is up to its neck in everything that is going on in Syria. The global jihad is also gaining strength in that arena,*" he explained. According to the top officer, Israel would soon "*encounter Hezbollah offensives, be it frontally or in the form of widespread combat within Lebanon.*"

Gantz also expressed concerns over the "dramatic" armament in the Gaza Strip. "*We have to maintain our superiority in the sea, on land and in the air, as well as in terms of intelligence*" Gantz said. He then turned his attention to Iran, reiterating Israel's mantra on the subject of a nuclear Iran. "*Iran has not relinquished its nuclear vision*" Gantz stated.

"*I am convinced that Iran must be stopped before it achieves nuclear power, which, in turn, will spark an arms race. With the help of the international community, we can make it so that Iran will never get there, be it by use of force or without use of force. Iran must not achieve nuclear power*" Gantz concluded.

170,000 missiles

Gen. Itay Baron, head of the Israeli army Military Intelligence research section, said "terrorist" organizations have been successfully rearming their missiles' stockpile for the past 18 months since the November 2012 Gaza operation Pillar of Defense.

In his address at the annual Herzliya Conference, Baron said that currently in Gaza there are hundreds of long-range missiles, which are aimed at the center of Israel.

Baron estimated that at any given moment there are 170,000 missiles aimed at Israel, mostly short-ranged ones. According to him, Iran plays a crucial part in helping the "terrorist" organizations arm themselves with more updated weapons. Addressing Hezbollah, Baron said the militant group is busy building deterrence against Israel, which includes arming itself with advanced missiles.

R&D Master

The improvements in Hezbollah's military and technological capacities can be owed, to an astonishing degree, to the work of one man: Hassan al-Laqis. One of Hezbollah's top innovators and technical minds, al-Laqis was assassinated in Beirut this past December by unknown assailants. While his murderers may remain mysterious, al-Laqis' legacy is clear: Hezbollah is now far ahead of any other terrorist group in the world in terms of the weapons it can deploy, the tactics it uses, and the offensive and defensive technology at its disposal. With the support of Iran, and the guidance of al-Laqis, Hezbollah is not a terrorist group, but rather Tehran's terrorist army.

The higher one goes up Hezbollah's military chain of command, the more secret and mysterious its members and activities become, and al-Laqis was no exception. His work was concealed even from many Hezbollah members, and he was granted relative independence in leading the organization's research and development division. He worked primarily on making Hezbollah's rocket and missile arsenal more accurate and deadly, its internal telecommunications systems more sophisticated and difficult to breach, and, most recently, spearheading efforts to develop Unmanned Aerial Vehicles (UAV), such as drones, for use in both offensive operations and intelligence gathering.

Although al-Laqis' assassination was clearly a setback for Hezbollah, his activities had already made substantial progress at the time of his death, and his life's work will threaten Israel for years to come. Under his supervision, Hezbollah went from being a standard-issue terrorist group employing crude tactics like suicide bombers and katyusha rockets to a technologically advanced paramilitary organization capable of accurately firing missiles at almost any Israeli target, especially civilian areas. The man may be gone, but the fruits of his labors remain.

Indeed, Hezbollah's capabilities have expanded across the board. Its arsenal has grown dramatically since 2006, in both quantity and quality. This includes mortars and small rockets with a range of 24 miles and, more disturbingly, rockets and missiles that can strike anywhere in Israel. Hezbollah is also believed to possess guided missiles accurate to within dozens of meters.

Fighting principles

This style of fighting is based on three principles: Absorption, deterrence, and attrition. Absorption refers to the organization's ability to withstand attack or retaliation. Hezbollah has sought to maximize its absorption capacities by building intricate systems of underground tunnels and bunkers across southern Lebanon, which it uses to store and transfer weapons and fighters from one combat zone to another, and as shelter from IDF retaliation. These bolt-holes also help create the sense of a "disappearing" enemy, difficult to detect and target. After all, you cannot defeat what you cannot see.

Hezbollah also deftly exploits the IDF's rules of engagement, which seek to safeguard civilian lives, by using densely populated urban areas to store and launch rockets. This strategy has a propaganda element as well. Hezbollah is well aware that Israel will be globally condemned if civilians are killed in the crossfire, as they almost inevitably will be given the use of such tactics. While often effective, this tactic is, in essence, a double war crime: Hezbollah fires rockets and missiles directly at Israeli civilians, while using the civilian population it rules as human shields; both of which are entirely illegal under international law.

In regard to deterrence and attrition, both refer to Hezbollah's ability to keep up its fight against Israel without suffering total destruction, thus drawing out the conflict to such an extent that it becomes difficult to bear the cost of sustaining it. Hezbollah's massive arsenal ensures that Israeli towns and civilians will suffer a constant barrage of rockets and missiles, something the director of IDF Intelligence has recently referred to as an "era of fire." In order to destroy this arsenal and the infrastructure used to deploy it, Israel needs a combined air, ground, and sea attack. To be successful, however, Israel will need to overcome Hezbollah's advanced anti-air and anti-ship weapons, countless booby traps and ambushes, abduction attempts, advanced anti-tank missiles, and many other challenges.

In addition, Israel will face intense domestic and international pressure to end the fighting as quickly as possible, while Hezbollah will seek to sustain it in order to inflict maximum damage. The organization has adopted this strategy because it believes that anything short of total military defeat—something that is all but impossible given its strategy of attrition—is a total victory for the organization. They also believe that this will create a sense of frustration and despair among Israelis, giving them the feeling that they cannot defeat such a ruthless, radical, and well-armed enemy.

Sectarian war

As a result, since 2006 Israel has sought to limit its operations against Hezbollah to avoid being drawn into a large-scale conflict. But this strategy is becoming obsolete due to factors within Lebanon itself. Although it is usually agreed that only the state should have a monopoly on the use of force, Hezbollah exercises this privilege throughout southern Lebanon, and its opponents treat it as such; as a result, domestic and foreign Sunni groups that support the Syrian rebels— including offshoots of al-Qaeda—have now taken the fight to Hezbollah on its own turf in Lebanon. The resulting sectarian violence has led to an ominous trend: The presence of Sunni jihadist groups in Lebanon is rising swiftly.

Israel's threat estimate

There are three principal security scenarios in the near future, former national security adviser Maj.-Gen. (res.) Yaakov Amidror has said, naming them as a large-scale ground war against Hezbollah in Lebanon, attrition against Hamas in Gaza, and the possibility of a military operation in Iran.

The military must prepare for these challenges while providing ongoing security, Amidror, a senior researcher at the Begin-Sadat Center for Strategic

Studies, said in a report published on the center's website. The feat *"will be neither easy nor cheap"* he added.

"The most significant threat to Israel's very existence is the possibility that some time in 2015, Iran will reach a deal with the West that would allow it to pursue some form of nuclear military capability. This process will not come to fruition this year, but a bad deal with the superpowers would be an important milestone for Tehran" Amidror warned.

"The strongest of them is Hezbollah, which was formed with a dual purpose in mind: It represents Iran's long reach in the area and against Israel, while at the same time it aims to control Lebanon, where the Shi'ites are the largest ethnic group. Hezbollah most closely resembles an army, and its arsenal totals some 150,000 missiles and rockets, several thousand of which can target any area in Israel. This rare and substantial firepower apparently even exceeded the firepower possessed by most of the European states combined" Amidror said in the report.

"Additionally, Hezbollah is armed with surface-to-sea missiles, anti-aircraft missiles, drones and modern anti-tank missiles. It is well organized into a military-style hierarchy and appears to possess command and control systems of high quality. It was established by Iranian leaders, but its leadership has always consisted of Lebanese people who were closely linked to Iran's interests" the report continued. *"Hezbollah assisted the Shi'ites by providing for their needs in the civilian sphere as a base for building its military power."*

Hezbollah is busy with its intervention in Syria, a war it deems crucial for its own survival, according to Amidror. *"It fights beside the Syrian Alawites because it needs them to stay in power. If Assad survives, Hezbollah's status in Lebanon will increase, as will its status in Damascus."*

Hamas

Hamas in the Gaza Strip also constitutes a steadily rising security threat, one that is able to manufacture its own long-range rockets and tunnel grid.

Hamas is left with 3,500 rockets after a 50-day war with Israel. Now, *"the big question is the speed at which Hamas can regain the capabilities it has lost. For Hamas, the current regime in Egypt is a formidable obstacle. Hamas has the markings of a well-organized military organization, as well as an impressive ability to learn and improve"* Amidror wrote.

Islamic Jihad in Gaza cannot be discounted as a threat either. Amidror noted that in 2015, no real army threatens Israel's security any longer. Egypt's military does not hold Israel as a prime target, and Egyptian military leaders have yet to consolidate their hold on power, the former national security adviser argued.

The Syrian army is completely engaged in the civil war, *"and while it still possesses a substantial arsenal, its units have been compromised, its morale is extremely low, and many of its commanders fear for their lives if the other side should win. The once enormous Iraqi army, at one time seen as having the ability to change the balance of power on the eastern front against Israel, has ceased to exist."*

Additionally, Amidror stated, *"the small but professional Jordanian army is looking east and north, toward the crumbling states of Iraq and Syria Islamist terrorists are thriving within the power vacuum in both countries, and Jordan may already be in their crosshairs."*

"Gulf states, led by Saudi Arabia, are arming themselves with the best of Western weaponry to prepare themselves for Iran. Radical jihadi elements are basing themselves in the Sinai Peninsula and Syrian Golan, but the threat they pose to Israel is less significant, due to their current lack of strength," he said.

Israel's dilemma

This violence is now threatening to spill over the Israeli border, which could make large-scale Israeli military action very difficult to avoid. For example, rockets have been fired across the Lebanese border in an apparent attempt to provoke IDF retaliation against Hezbollah. The explosive potential of such attacks is enormous. If one rocket from Lebanon strikes an Israeli city and causes casualties, Israel would have no choice but to retaliate. In turn, this could draw Hezbollah and Israel into a new round of conflict, potentially as large and as difficult as that in 2006. To say the least, this is an outcome that the Israeli military and political establishments want to avoid.

Obviously, Israel could attempt to destroy Hezbollah by launching a military operation much larger and more comprehensive than that of 2006. Theoretically, such a war could be successful. But in practice, it would likely be impossible. In order to achieve victory, the operation would have to be relatively long, and Israel would almost certainly be forced to end it prematurely due to domestic and international pressure.

In the present diplomatic climate, no major world power, not even the United States, is willing to risk significant diplomatic capital in order to destroy Iranian proxies—even those it considers to be terrorists. At best, Israel could temporarily retard Hezbollah's military capabilities. At worst, a failed campaign could further enhance Hezbollah's prestige and position in Lebanon.

Some believe that Hezbollah will eventually moderate on its own. This seems unlikely, especially since it continues to operate with impunity while its military capabilities only expand. If anything, the group appears to be becoming more radical, more violent, and more dangerous. Hezbollah feels strong and will not compromise from a position of strength.

Certainly, the IDF will continue to use limited force in order to contain the threat from Hezbollah; but the problem cannot be conclusively resolved unless the group itself is contained. This can only be accomplished through diplomatic action and political pressure on both Hezbollah and its patrons in Iran. Israel and its supporters, then, should make substantial efforts to persuade the international community to adopt the policies outlined above. Without such efforts, there is little chance of bringing peace to Israel's northern border—or of defanging the most significant force for projecting Iranian might against Western interests today.